Social Issues
in Literature

Civil Rights in Richard Wright's *Native Son*

Other Books in the Social Issues in Literature Series:

Social Issues
in Literature

Civil Rights in Richard Wright's *Native Son*

Candice L. Mancini, Book Editor

GREENHAVEN PRESS
A part of Gale, Cengage Learning

Detroit • New York • San Francisco • New Haven, Conn • Waterville, Maine • London

Christine Nasso, *Publisher*
Elizabeth Des Chenes, *Managing Editor*

For more information, contact:
Greenhaven Press
27500 Drake Rd.
Farmington Hills, MI 48331-3535
Or you can visit our Internet site at gale.cengage.com

For product information and technology assistance, contact us at

Gale Customer Support, 1-800-877-4253
For permission to use material from this text or product, submit all requests online at www.cengage.com/permissions

Further permissions questions can be emailed to permissionrequest@cengage.com

Articles in Greenhaven Press anthologies are often edited for length to meet page requirements. In addition, original titles of these works are changed to clearly present the main thesis and to explicitly indicate the author's opinion. Every effort is made to ensure that Greenhaven Press accurately reflects the original intent of the authors. Every effort has been made to trace the owners of copyrighted material.

Cover photograph © Hulton Archive/Getty Images.

LIBRARY OF CONGRESS CATALOGING-IN-PUBLICATION DATA

Civil Rights in Richard Wright's Native Son / Candice L. Mancini, book editor.
   p. cm. -- (Social issues in literature)
  Includes bibliographical references and index.
  ISBN 978-0-7377-4392-0 (hardcover)
  ISBN 978-0-7377-4391-3 (pbk.)
  1. Wright, Richard, 1908-1960. 2. Native son. 3. Civil rights in literature. I. Mancini, Candice.
  PS3545.R815N3366 2009
  813'.52--dc22

                                             2008055431

Printed in the United States of America
1 2 3 4 5 6 7 13 12 11 10 09

Contents

Chapter 1: Background on Richard Wright

Edward D. Clark

Richard Wright was one of the most important writers in American history. His writing reflects themes of urban plight and racial discrimination and forced whites to see the reality of black American life.

Hazel Rowley

As a young adult, Wright lived in Chicago, where he encountered different relations between blacks and whites than he had in the South. But even in the North, racism persisted.

Chapter 2: *Native Son* and Civil Rights

James Baldwin

As a protest novel, *Native Son* focuses on anarchy in society, for which Bigger was a symbol. But the novel ignores the complexities of African American life, including its traditions and relationships.

Irving Howe

Some criticism of *Native Son* is too harsh and fails to see how the novel forever changed American culture by forcing whites to see the results of their oppression and blacks the cost of their submission.

Chapter 3: Contemporary Perspectives on Civil Rights

Introduction

Bigger Thomas wanted control over his life. He wanted the right to go where he desired, live where he desired. He wanted to fly a plane. Bigger did not delude himself: He was aware that his status as a black man living in the 1930s United States prevented him from attaining these things. But this did not make it easy to accept. "I know I oughtn't think about it," Bigger told his pal Gus, "but I can't help it. Every time I think about it I feel like somebody's poking a red-hot iron down my throat. . . . Half the time I feel like I'm on the outside of the world peeping in through a knot-hole in the fence." As far as Bigger could see, whites had everything and he had nothing. "They own the world," he told Gus. When he began working for the Daltons, this feeling was confirmed in Bigger. The Daltons were millionaires with a beautiful house, a car, servants.

But the Daltons were created by a man who did not exactly rejoice in capitalist excess. Richard Wright was a member of the American Communist Party during the time he wrote *Native Son*. And it was from his perspective as a socialist, perhaps as much as from his perspective as a black man, that Wright authored his novel. In creating Mr. Dalton, Wright personified society's idea of the quintessential American philanthropist. As Mr. Dalton pointed out to Bigger, he was a supporter of the National Association for the Advancement of Colored People (NAACP), and his wife had "a very deep interest in colored people." But this was not how Wright perceived the Daltons when he created them. It is true that Mrs. Dalton portrayed sensitivity and a desire to help African Americans, especially in her desire to help them achieve an education. But it was no coincidence that Mrs. Dalton was physically blind: her perception of blacks was based on her own experiences, and she made no attempt to understand them as individuals.

As for Mr. Dalton, although he donated money to the NAACP, he exploited the very same people he helped. The owner of low-income housing, Mr. Dalton charged his black renters higher prices than he did whites for identical apartments. When Bigger's attorney, Boris Max, pointed this out during Bigger's trial, Mr. Dalton claimed he was not to blame. It was "the law of supply and demand that regulates the price of houses," he explained. In other words, because the black section of the city was more crowded than the white section, and because blacks were not allowed to rent in the white section, the demand for rentals in the black side of town was higher, leading to higher prices. According to Mr. Dalton, this was all beyond his control, even though he was the very one who owned these properties and received the rental money they generated.

While Wright was certainly questioning society's segregation of blacks, he also was questioning capitalism's justification of exploitation. With Mr. Dalton, Wright was emphasizing how even philanthropists allowed the law of capitalism to lead their decision making, even if it meant their capitalistic actions contradicted their humanitarian ones. As Wright made clear, such acts of capitalism have damaged African Americans in more ways than by making them victims of poverty and exploitation. To Wright, further damage occurred when blacks desired to play the roles of the very people who oppressed them. In *Native Son*, this desire was plainly demonstrated through Bigger and Gus's game, "Playing White."

In 1964, four years after Wright's death, the Civil Rights Act was passed, granting African Americans equal protection of the laws and banning segregation in public spaces. But more than forty years later, African Americans continue to experience poverty, unemployment, and incarceration at higher rates than whites. How would Wright view this current situation, if he were still alive? Would he maintain that, first and foremost, such is the case because racism persists? Or would he argue that the flaws of capitalism must share the blame?

The current hip-hop culture brings such questions to light. Some hip-hop values, such as its long-criticized emphasis on materialism, seem in direct contrast with those Wright endorsed in *Native Son*. Although much of hip-hop rails against society, especially white society, by focusing on material possessions it embraces the very establishment it criticizes. But some hip-hop artists recognize and critique this. For example, just as Richard Wright saw Bigger as the brutal result of the racist and capitalist culture in which he lived, hip-hop artist Kanye West blames hip-hop's materialism on present-day society:

> It seems we living the American
> dream
>
> But the people highest up got the
> lowest self esteem
>
> The prettiest people do the ugliest
> things
>
> For the road to riches and dia-
> mond rings
>
> (West, "All Falls Down," 2004)

The following essays investigate the denial of civil rights to African Americans as revealed in Wright's *Native Son* and examine how the issue continues to have impact today.

Chronology

1908

Richard Nathaniel Wright is born on September 4, in the rural outskirts of Natchez, Mississippi.

1911

Wright's brother, Leon Alan, is born. The family, unable to support themselves through farming, move in with Wright's maternal grandparents in Natchez, where Wright catches his grandparents' house on fire.

1913–1914

In search of better employment, the Wright family moves to Memphis, Tennessee. Here, Nathan Wright meets another woman and abandons his family. Ella Wright works as a cook to support the family.

1915

In September, Wright begins school at Memphis's Howe Institute.

1916

Ella Wright contracts a terrible illness. Wright's grandmother comes to Memphis to care for the family. For a month after she leaves, Wright and his brother are placed in Settlement House, an orphanage. After this, they move in with their maternal grandparents, who now live in Jackson, Mississippi. From here, they move in with Wright's Aunt Maggie and Uncle Silas Hoskins in Elaine, Arkansas.

1917–1918

Wright's Uncle Silas is murdered by whites, and the family flees, first to Helena, Arkansas, next to Jackson, Mississippi, and then back to Helena. As a result of these moves, Wright's education is sporadic. Ella Wright, whose health has temporarily improved enough for her to work, cooks and cleans for whites.

1918–1919

Wright begins school in the fall of 1918, but in early 1919 must leave early because Ella Wright's health is again failing and he must earn money for the family. Ella suffers a stroke, and the family moves back to Jackson.

1921–1925

This period marks a time of serious racial discrimination throughout the United States. The Ku Klux Klan becomes more widespread, and racial riots increase in frequency. Wright manages to get through school, working odd jobs, and graduates valedictorian of ninth grade. Wright completes his first short story, "The Voodoo of Hell's Half-Acre." Wright begins high school, but quits after a few weeks to earn more money. In November 1925, at the age of seventeen, Wright moves to Memphis, Tennessee.

1927

In December, Wright moves with his Aunt Maggie to Chicago.

1928

Wright works in a grocery store and at a restaurant, and then finds temporary work with the post office. Wright's mother and brother move in with him and Aunt Maggie; later, Wright's Aunt Cleopatra joins them. Wright is denied a permanent position with the postal service because he fails the medical examination.

1929

Wright passes the postal health exam, after forcing himself to eat large amounts of food. He begins work as a substitute clerk and mail sorter.

1930

Wright loses his job at the post office, but he finds work as an aide at the South Side Boys Club. He also works with the Federal Negro Theatre and becomes a writer for the Illinois Writer's Project. Wright begins work on *Cesspool.*

1932–1933

Wright tries to support his family by selling insurance policies, but fails. He works as a street cleaner and finds temporary holiday work at the post office. He joins the Chicago John Reed Club, a literary organization sponsored by the Communist Party, where he serves as secretary. He is published in the John Reed Club's *Left Front* publication.

1934

Wright officially joins the Communist Party and continues to publish in left-leaning journals.

1936

Wright helps to organize the South Side Writer's Group. "Big Boy Leaves Home" is published in the *New Negro Caravan.*

1937

Wright moves to New York and becomes Harlem editor of the *Daily Worker*, a Communist newspaper. His story "Fire and Cloud" wins first prize in the *Story Magazine* contest.

1938

Wright's *Uncle Tom's Children* is published.

1939

Wright wins a Guggenheim Fellowship of $2,500 and finishes *Native Son*. In August, he marries Dhima Rose Meadman.

1940

Native Son is published as a Book-of-the-Month Club selection. After a month, it has sold more than 215,000 copies and is a best seller.

1941

Wright is awarded the Spingarn Medal by the NAACP. After divorcing Dhima Rose Meadman, Wright marries Ellen Poplar, a white woman.

1942

After years of struggles with the Communist Party, Wright splits from the organization. *12 Million Black Voices* is published.

1945

Black Boy is published.

1946

Wright moves to France in order to escape the persistent racism he faces in the United States.

1953

Wright's *The Outsider* is published. He visits present-day Ghana to observe a country freeing itself from colonial rule.

1954

Wright's *Savage Holiday* is published.

1956

Wright helps organize the First Congress of Negro Artists and Writers in Paris.

1957

Wright publishes the nonfiction book *White Man, Listen!*.

1958

Wright's *The Long Dream* is published.

1959

Wright is denied a resident visa by British officials, even after his wife and daughters move to England. His health begins to decline.

1960

Wright begins a new novel, *A Father's Law,* and finishes *Eight Men.* Failing health brings him in and out of hospitals. On November 28, Wright dies from a heart attack while at a Paris hospital for gastrointestinal problems. On December 3, his body is cremated with a copy of *Black Boy* at the Pere Lachaise cemetery.

1963

Wright's first novel, *Cesspool,* which was never published, is re-titled as *Lawd Today!* and published posthumously.

CHAPTER 1

Background on
Richard Wright

The Life of Richard Wright

Edward D. Clark

Edward D. Clark taught at North Carolina State University at the time he wrote this article.

Born in rural Mississippi and moving to Memphis as a child, Richard Wright faced extreme racial prejudice while growing up. After moving to Chicago at the age of nineteen, Wright experienced a different kind of racism than he had in the South, but it was racism, nonetheless. Eventually, after his writing career showed great success, Wright chose to make France his home because of his growing dissatisfaction with racial policies in the United States. His writing career followed a series of successes and drawbacks, yet Richard Wright was one of the most influential African American writers.

Any serious discussion of the development of black fiction in modern American literature must include Richard Wright. He was the first black novelist to describe the plight of the urban masses and the first to present this material in the naturalistic tradition. Not only is he the father of the post–World War II black novel, he is also the main precursor of the black arts movement of the 1960s. Ralph Ellison and James Baldwin are but two of many outstanding black writers who profited from his influence. Moreover, he was, as Robert Felgar explains in *Richard Wright* (1980), "perhaps the very first writer to give the white community explanations and themes that cut through its prejudices and forced it to look at the reality of black life in America."

Richard Nathaniel Wright felt victimized by racial discrimination and racial prejudice throughout his life in the

United States. He experienced some of the most severe abuses of racial oppression in Mississippi, where he was born on 4 September 1908, on a plantation in Roxie twenty-two miles east of Natchez, to sharecropper Nathan Wright and teacher Ella Wilson Wright. Nathan Wright, like most black sharecroppers, was extremely poor. In 1911 Ella Wright went to Natchez to live with her family while Nathan became an itinerant worker. Later that same year, in an effort to improve their economic status, Nathan Wright loaded his family onto a riverboat at Natchez and migrated to Memphis, Tennessee. Nathan Wright then deserted his family.

Richard Wright lived in Memphis until he was almost eight. As small children he and his younger brother Leon were often hungry and were expected to look out for themselves. The menial jobs that Ella Wright now had to take did not provide adequate income to support the family. Wright's autobiography, *Black Boy* (1945), explains: "I would feel hunger nudging my ribs, twisting my empty guts until they ached. I would grow dizzy and my vision would dim." His mother would send him to beg money from his father, now living with a mistress. In 1914 Ella Wright became ill, and the two brothers were sent to Settlement House, a Methodist orphanage.

An Irregular Education

Mrs. Wright and her sons moved to Elaine, Arkansas, to live with her sister, Maggie, and Maggie's husband, Silas Hoskins, in the summer of 1916. In late 1916 or early 1917 Silas Hoskins was murdered by whites who coveted his property, and the family fled to West Helena, Arkansas, where they lived in fear in rented rooms for several weeks. Mrs. Wright took the boys to Jackson, Mississippi, for several months in 1917, but they returned to West Helena by the winter of 1918. Further family disintegration occurred after Mrs. Wright suffered a stroke in 1919. Wright reluctantly chose to live with Uncle Clark and

Richard Wright in front of posters of the film Sangre Negra *at the Venice Film Festival in Venice, Italy, August 22, 1951. Wright starred in the Argentine film, which was based on his novel,* Native Son. *AP Images.*

Aunt Jody in Greenwood, Mississippi, where he could be near his mother, but restrictions placed on him by his aunt and uncle made him an emotional wreck. On the verge of a nervous breakdown, he was permitted to return to Jackson, where he lived with Grandmother Wilson from early 1920 until late 1925.

Wright's education was greatly disrupted by family disorganization. The frequent moves and Mrs. Wright's illness made regular school attendance impossible. Wright first entered Howe Institute in Memphis, Tennessee, around 1916. In 1920 he enrolled and remained for a year at the Seventh Day Adventist school in Jackson, Mississippi, with his Aunt Addie, a fanatical Seventh Day Adventist, the only teacher. Wright felt stifled by his aunt and his maternal grandmother, who tried to force him to pray that he might find God. He later threatened to leave home because Grandmother Wilson refused to permit him to work on Saturdays, the Adventist Sabbath. Early strife with his aunt and grandmother left him with a permanent, uncompromising hostility toward religious solutions to mundane problems. Traces of this hostility surface in much of his writing.

Wright's first formal education started in September 1921 when he joined a fifth grade class at Jim Hill Public School, Jackson, Mississippi. Within two weeks he was promoted to the sixth grade. In 1923 he enrolled at the Smith-Robinson School, also in Jackson; because of excellent grades he was made part-time supervisor of the class. Wright also showed special interest in and talent for writing, getting his first story, "The Voodoo of Hell's Half Acre," published in 1924 in the *Southern Register*, a black Jackson newspaper. In 1925 Wright was made class valedictorian. Determined not to be called an Uncle Tom [blacks who were reputed to be especially subservient to whites], he refused to deliver the assistant principal's carefully prepared valedictory address that would not offend the white school officials and finally convinced the black administrators to let him read essentially what he had written. In September of the same year Wright registered for mathematics, English, and history courses at the new Lanier High School in Jackson but had to stop attending classes after a few weeks of irregular attendance because he needed to earn money for family expenses.

Important Moves Accelerate Writing Career

In November 1925 Wright returned to Memphis with plans to get money to make "the first lap of a journey to a land where [he] could live with a little less fear." The two years he remained in Memphis were especially important, for there he indulged a developing passion for reading. He discovered *Harper's* magazine, the *Atlantic Monthly*, and the *American Mercury*. Through subterfuge he was able to borrow books from the white library. Of special importance to him were H.L. Mencken's *A Book of Prefaces* (1917) and one of his six volumes of *Prejudices* (1919–1927). Wright was particularly impressed with Mencken's vision of the South as hell.

Late in 1927 Wright arrived in Chicago, where he spent a decade that was as important to his development as his nineteen years in the South were. After finally securing employment as a postal clerk, he read other writers and studied their styles during his time off. His job at the post office eliminated by the Great Depression, he went on relief in 1931. In 1932 he began attending meetings of the Chicago John Reed Club, a Communist literary organization whose supposed purpose was to use art for revolutionary ends. Especially interested in the literary contacts made at the meetings, Wright formally joined the Communist party in late 1933 and as a revolutionary poet wrote numerous proletarian poems ("I Have Seen Black Hands," "We of the Streets," "Red Leaves of Red Books," for example) for *New Masses* and other left-wing periodicals.

By 1935 Wright had completed his first novel, "Cesspool," published as *Lawd Today* (1963), and in January 1936 his story "Big Boy Leaves Home" was accepted for publication in *New Caravan*. In February Wright began working with the National Negro Congress, and in April he chaired the South Side Writers' Group, whose membership included [African-American poets] Arna Bontemps and Margaret Walker. Wright submitted some of his critical essays and poetry to the group for criticism and read aloud some of his short stories. In 1936 he was also revising "Cesspool."

The year 1937 was a landmark for Wright. After a quarrel with a Communist party leader, he severed ties with the Chicago branch and went to New York in late May to become Harlem editor of the *Daily Worker*. Wright was also upset over repeated rejections of "Cesspool" and other works. He was happy that during his first year in New York all of his activities involved writing of some kind. In the summer and fall he wrote over two hundred articles for the *Daily Worker*. He helped organize *New Challenge*, a quarterly for works of progressive black authors, and wrote for the first issue "Blueprint for Negro Writing," the most complete and profound statement of his theories on Afro-American writing. Wright also wrote articles for *New Masses*, helped with the New York City Writers' Project, and continued revising the stories that would comprise *Uncle Tom's Children* (1938). The year was also a landmark for Wright because he met and developed a friendship with Ellison that would last for years, and he learned that he would receive the *Story* magazine first prize of five hundred dollars for his short story "Fire and Cloud."

Wright completed his final revision of "Cesspool" in 1937, and he was again disappointed that he could not get a publisher. This heavily-autobiographical first novel, published posthumously, is in some ways more structurally sophisticated than some of Wright's later works. The dreams, fantasies, and conscious behavior of its protagonist are the roots for later Wright themes: black nationalism, problems associated with mid-twentieth-century migration of blacks from the rural South to the industrial urban areas, and the absurdities of the existentialist hero. . . .

Literary Success

The publication and favorable reception of *Uncle Tom's Children* improved Wright's status with the Communist party and

enabled him to establish a reasonable degree of financial sta-
bility. He was appointed to the editorial board of *New Masses*,
and Granville Hicks, prominent literary critic and Communist
sympathizer, introduced him at leftist teas in Boston. By 6
May 1938 excellent sales had provided him with enough
money to move to Harlem, where he began writing *Native
Son* (1940).

In 1939 Wright met two white women who, he thought,
met his criteria for a wife: Dhimah Rose Meadman and Ellen
Poplar. He married Dhimah in August 1939 with Ralph Ellison as best man. The honeymoon was delayed until the spring
of 1940. During the honeymoon in Cuernavaca, Mexico,
Wright discovered how little he and Dhimah had in common,
and they left Mexico separately, never to be reconciled. After
his divorce from Dhimah, Wright married Ellen Poplar on 12
March 1941. Their first daughter Julia was born on 15 April
1942.

On the strength of *Uncle Tom's Children* and his comple-
tion of a section of *Native Son*, in early 1939 Wright was
awarded a Guggenheim Fellowship, which made it possible for
him to complete *Native Son* for publication by 1 March 1940.
The publication of the novel marked the beginning of a black
literature that refused to compromise with many white
expectations. . . .

Native Son sold two hundred thousand copies in under
three weeks, breaking a twenty-year record at Harper. Clifton
Fadiman in the *New Yorker* compared Wright to [writers]
Theodore Dreiser and John Steinbeck and praised his "passion
and intelligence" that examined "layers of consciousness only
[Russian novelist Fyodor] Dostoyevski and a few others have
penetrated." Henry S. Canby in *Book of the Month Club News*
wrote that, "like *Grapes of Wrath* it is a fully realized story . . .
uncompromisingly realistic and quite as human as it is Negro." Ralph Ellison in *New Masses* found in it "an artistry, pen-
etration of thought and sheer emotional power that places it

in the first rank of American fiction." Jonathan Daniels, Malcolm Cowley, Sterling Brown, and most other eminent black and white critics of the day praised the novel. The few dissenting voices, among them Howard Mumford Jones and David Cohn, had objections that were more personal than literary. While there is yet much critical debate over the place *Native Son* should occupy in the corpus of great literature, there is a consensus that the novel is one of the classic works of American literature. . . .

The remainder of 1945 and the years 1946 and 1947 were extremely busy and highly critical periods for Wright. He traveled abroad, delivered speeches, engaged in debates, reviewed books, and continued to write. In the fall of 1945 he toured the nation delivering lectures about the racial situation. He gave financial aid to black novelist Chester Himes and secured a grant for James Baldwin. He sailed for Paris on 1 May 1946, where he was lionized by the French press and private citizens. In Paris he became friends with [writer] Gertrude Stein and many French intellectuals, including Jean-Paul Sartre and Simone de Beauvoir. Wright and Ellen visited Switzerland in November, where he gave interviews and contacted a publisher for the German edition of *Black Boy*. In late 1946 Wright met George Padmore in London. Padmore, the father of African liberation, introduced him to the progressive, militant leaders of the Third World. This meeting had two significant and long-range effects upon Wright. His friendship with Padmore influenced his political thinking and further increased his interest in Africa. Meeting black leaders from all of the English-speaking African countries indicated to Wright that black America's call for freedom was now being echoed throughout the other nonwhite continents of the world, and he concluded that he must visit nonwhite countries.

By January 1947, when the family returned to Manhattan, Wright had become even more dissatisfied with American racial policies. He constantly contrasted the freedom and acceptance he experienced in Paris against the rampant racism he faced in America. Like [Irish writer] James Joyce, he felt that he could not expand his artistic and personal freedom unless he exiled himself from the oppressive soil of his native country. Wright and his family returned to Paris in August 1947 and became permanent citizens. Although Wright traveled extensively, France was his home base until his death in 1960. The last fourteen years of his life are especially notable for a shift in ideological emphases: instead of determinism he explored choice; along with racism he emphasized a more metaphysical isolation; in place of colonialism in the Deep South he focused on global oppression. Existentialism and identification with the people of the Third World are outgrowths of his earlier experiences. Though no longer a card-carrying Communist, his writings still reflect Marxist ideals and sympathies.

Life in the North

Hazel Rowley

In addition to writing a biography about Richard Wright, Hazel Rowley has published biographies of Simone de Beauvoir, Jean-Paul Sartre, and Christina Stead.

Richard Wright moved from Memphis to Chicago in 1927 at the age of nineteen. Hazel Rowley offers that Wright's early experiences in the North were mixed. On one hand, he felt he had accomplished much by moving out of the South and to Chicago, where he felt everything was possible. On the other hand, he found that although Chicago allowed more freedoms for African Americans than did the South, blacks were still discriminated against in jobs, education, and public spaces. In addition to Wright's struggles with northern racism, this period in his life was marked by family difficulties.

[At the age of nineteen, in 1927, Richard Wright moved to Chicago, where he] rented a room in the same tenement house as his Aunt Cleo. The next day, Wright took the streetcar south until he could see no more black faces, then got off and walked, looking for work. A sign in the window of a delicatessen read: "Porter Wanted." A stout woman with a thick European accent told him he would have to wait for her husband, and he realized, with a faint shock, that they were Jewish, the same people he and his friends used to taunt when they were young. He got the job and the work proved easy, but his ears were unaccustomed to European accents and he often had no idea what his bosses were saying to him. The woman, particularly, was impatient with him. When he once ventured to ask her to write something down so he could *see* what she was saying, she shouted at him that she could not write. He felt humiliated. He had to be patient with her broken English; why couldn't she be more patient with him, an outsider from the South? "Only one answer came to my mind. I was black and she did not care." Later, he realized how wrong he had been about this Jewish couple, the first white people he had ever met who treated him like an equal. In this Northern city, the interaction between blacks and whites was utterly perplexing to him.

Black workers were kept out of most skilled jobs. Factory managers preferred white immigrants. Wright soon learned that the best job for black male workers—indeed, the only "clerical" job available to them—was at the Chicago post office. It was an unskilled job, but comparatively well paid, and it was possible to be promoted to a permanent position. The entrance examination involved committing to memory a "scheme" of nine hundred white cards, with place names and zip code numbers. An entrance exam was coming up, and Wright studied hard. He decided he would need two days off work: one for last-minute preparation, and one to sit the exam. Could he be honest with his bosses? He chose not to risk it. They might be angry, and he needed his wages.

For two days he did not turn up to work. Feeling guilty when he went back, he overcompensated with a tall story about his mother just having died in Memphis. His bosses did not believe him, and they were hurt that he was lying to them. In his embarrassment, Wright insisted all the more fervently that he was telling the truth. He felt like a child. At the end of the week he collected his wages and never went back. "I just wanted to go quickly and have them forget that I had ever worked for them."

While he waited to hear from the post office, he got a job as an errand boy and dishwasher in a North Side café. The hours were long, but the pay, at fifteen dollars a week, was higher than most casual jobs. And in the late afternoons he carried dinner trays to people in the nearby hotel, which brought in tips. This was the place—he writes about it in *Black Boy*—where he discovered that the cook, a tall, red-faced Finnish woman admired for her culinary skills, regularly spat into the pot of soup she had boiling on the stove. Wright did not know what to do. Would the "boss lady" believe him—a black man denouncing a white woman? For weeks he kept the knowledge to himself. When the café employed a young black waitress, he confided in her. They agreed she should tell the boss—a black woman had a better chance of being believed than a black man—and that they were prepared to be fired. In fact, the cook was shown the door.

Neither Color nor Blood

Wright found the young white waitresses "hard" and "brisk" compared with the women down South, but unlike Southern women, they were "relatively free of the heritage of racial hate." One day, one of them squeezed against him to draw a cup of coffee. She seemed to think nothing of it. Another morning, a waitress came rushing in late, and asked him to tie her apron. For Wright, these moments were seared with significance. He had never before come in close contact with a white woman, and these encounters were "charged with the memory of dread." It was a balm to his taut nerves to discover that in the North not all white women shrank from him as "a creature to be avoided at all costs."

At lunchtime he would sit on a bench in a nearby park. Sometimes two or three of the waitresses joined him. They would smoke cigarettes and chat. After eighteen years in which he had done little more than exchange polite phrases with white people, he found himself listening to these young women talk about their hopes for the future, their home lives, their boyfriends. He was struck by the shallowness of their emotions and their "tawdry dreams" of material acquisition. It seemed to him that black people lived "a truer and deeper life."

A portrait of Wright in his New York study, May 1943. Wright moved to New York in 1936, after living in Chicago for ten years. The Library of Congress.

Another thought took hold of him as he listened to the chatter of those waitresses. If white Americans were ever going to reach any kind of emotional maturity, they needed to know about Negro lives. He would tell the stories that black people were rarely capable of telling themselves. He would make white readers understand that the differences between black and white folk were not about blood or color. He would try to show that "Negroes are Negroes because they are treated as Negroes."

Northern Racism

At other times he worried that these thoughts of his were merely "fantasies of ambition" that prevented him from drowning in a "sea of senselessness." He was still in a state of shock. Down South, his entire existence had been focused on the idea of getting away to the North. There had even been a kind of quiet satisfaction in knowing himself on the outside of Southern life, for he had plans to travel beyond that world. In his mind, Chicago had represented "a place where everything was possible." He had told himself that once in that Northern city, he would go back to school and write books. Now he was there and he was seeing just how finite the possibilities were. He had left behind the racist brutality of the South, but the humiliations of the North were almost harder to bear, because they were more capricious. Chicago had once been known for its unusually fair attitude toward its black citizens, but the vast influx of black peasants unfamiliar with city ways had strained race relations. Southern whites had also come to the North in pursuit of jobs, and they brought their race hatred with them. Never quite knowing what was permitted and what was not, black people in the North were left in a constant state of possible infraction.

It was true that blacks and whites jostled each other on the El [elevated train] and the streetcars; they mingled at ballparks, in retail stores, and in the city's cheaper or chain restaurants; blacks could sit in the public libraries and visit the city's museums. But other places had a rigid color line. Even on Forty-seventh Street, the main commercial strip of Bronzeville, the more pretentious restaurants, nightclubs, and cocktail lounges did not allow blacks inside the door. Many parks and swimming pools across the city were closed to blacks. Even the cool waters of Lake Michigan were often out of bounds. (The 1919 race riots in Chicago were set off when a black boy was stoned by white boys at one of the beaches on the shores of Lake Michigan when he crossed the "imaginary line.") Most hotels were closed to blacks seeking rooms; some movie houses refused to allow blacks on the main floor. Bowling alleys, roller-skating rinks, and public dance halls were segregated. The universities officially accepted black students (Northwestern had forty in a student body of eleven thousand); but they were not allowed in the student café, they could not live in the dorms, they could not use the college pool, and where were the decent jobs for them when they qualified?

In *Lawd Today!* [a novel Wright wrote in the 1930s but was not published until 1963, after his death] the black postal workers no longer have any illusions about the North: "The only difference between the North and the South is, them guys down there'll kill you, and these up here'll let you starve to death," one says to another. His friend rationalizes: "Well, I'd rather die slow than to die fast!"

Struggles with Work and Home

With tips, Wright's weekly income at the café came to around twenty dollars. He put aside as much as possible. [His Aunt] Maggie, who was working as a pieceworker in the garment industry, rented a two-room apartment, and Richard moved in. They decided to summon [his mother] Ella and [his brother] Leon from Memphis. For months, Richard shared the windowless rear room with his mother and brother.

The arrangement was bound to cause tension. Wright was almost twenty. In the last couple of years he had enjoyed a measure of autonomy and privacy. For the next nine years he would find himself confined in close quarters with his mother, his aunt—and before long, his grandmother. These women brought with them the values of the Southern black community he had so fervently wanted to escape. "The consciousness of vast sections of our black women lies beyond the boundaries of the modern world," he would write in *12 Million Black Voices*.

In June 1928 he was called for temporary work at the post office. At seventy cents an hour, he came away from the eight-hour shift with $5.60. His spirits soared. With a regular clerical position at the post office, he would be able to spend at least five hours every day reading and writing. The only obstacle was the physical examination. It carried a minimum weight requirement: a male had to weigh 125 pounds or more. Wright weighed 110 pounds. For weeks, he crammed food into himself, buying milk and steak as an investment for the future. To his despair, his weight did not change. A doctor told him it would take time to make up for the years of malnutrition. He failed the physical.

Close Living Quarters

His mother became sick again. Maggie, struggling to bring in money, was incensed by the sight of her nephew reading. She saw it as idleness, which led nowhere. It swelled the electric bill and was not going to help him find a job. Throughout Richard's childhood she had been his sole supporter in the family; now she too was coming around to the idea that he was marked for failure. Doubtless, Wright was taunted with the sorts of comments Bigger Thomas hears from his family in *Native Son*: "We wouldn't have to live in this garage dump if you had any manhood in you." The bickering became ugly. Finally Wright decided he would put up with it no more; he did not want a reenactment of his domestic life in Jackson. His Aunt Maggie could go her own way.

He managed to get himself reemployed by the North Side café, and though he had no savings whatsoever, he rented a room and a kitchen for the family, and this time asked his

Aunt Cleo to join them. "Aunt Sissie," as the family called her, was to stay with them for the duration of Richard's time in Chicago.

Richard and Leon slept in the kitchen, where the smell of cooking never went away. The place was infested with cockroaches and bedbugs, and the more they scrubbed the place and doused it with kerosene and insect powder, the more the vermin seemed to multiply. Wright willed himself away from his dismal surroundings by reading [Marcel Proust's] *A Remembrance of Things Past* for hours each night. He was "stupefied by its dazzling magic" and crushed by the thought he could never write about the people in his environment like Proust did.

Forging a Writing Life

Writing had become his single aim in life. Without the slightest encouragement from anyone, he devoured books. He studied the writer's craft, sentence by sentence, paragraph by paragraph. Then he covered sheets of paper with his own efforts. Imitating the masters, he tried to construct sentences like theirs. He could see that a good sentence not only conveyed meaning but also the feel of something—the mood. "The lump of butter melted slowly and seeped down the golden grooves of the yam." He was pleased with that sentence. Generally he tore up his pages of writing, swearing to do better in the future.

Leon viewed his brother's reading and writing with "a distant and baffled curiosity." Their mother ignored it. Aunt Cleo would watch Wright for a while as he pored over his books, then shake her head. Their relatives in Chicago, cousins of his mother and aunts, were equally nonplussed. Wright rarely attended family gatherings.

In the spring of 1929 he took the post office physical examination again. This time he met the required weight. For the first time, his situation looked promising. The family moved to a four-room apartment at 4831 Vincennes Avenue. Wright paid fifty dollars a month in rent, more than he had ever paid in his life. He was proud of himself. "At last my mother had a place she could call her own after a fashion."

Like most of the temporary clerks, he was put on the night shift. He and his friends would come stumbling out at 4:30 A.M. Once in a blue moon, Wright would go with them to a "speakeasy" for what they called a "daycap" before going home to sleep. His precious afternoon hours were spent read-ing—often in the public library uptown. Still using [social commentator H.L.] Mencken's *Book of Prefaces* as his guide, he read [Anton] Chekhov, [Anton] Turgenev, and [Guy de] Maupassant. He was marked by Stephen Crane's novel *Maggie: A Girl of the Streets*, about an innocent girl in the seedy New York tenement district who briefly becomes a prostitute and finally commits suicide.

How, he asked himself, would [Émile] Zola, [Theodore] Dreiser, and Crane write about the South Side? He wanted to apply their seemingly impartial naturalistic techniques to de-pict the daily lives of black people. But he was serving a be-wildering apprenticeship, without a guide or fellow writer in sight. Sometimes he felt quite desperate about the chasm be-tween his ambitions and his everyday reality.

Social Issues
in Literature

CHAPTER 2

Native Son and Civil Rights

A Protest Novel

James Baldwin

James Baldwin (1924–1987) was an African American writer who published four novels and three essay collections.

Native Son was the first novel to paint the true picture of what it was like to be black in America. The novel was closely intertwined with the social climate in which it existed: it was published a year before the start of the Second World War, a time when the memory of the Depression was painfully close and when Communist ideologies ran rampant in the United States. These struggles only magnified the difficulties of African Americans, who too recently had been enslaved. Wright's character of Bigger Thomas was symbolic of these struggles. Yet, James Baldwin writes, the reader is so limited to Bigger's perspective that the layers of true African American life and traditions are not present in the novel.*

The most powerful and celebrated statement we have yet had of what it means to be a Negro in America is unquestionably Richard Wright's *Native Son*. The feeling which prevailed at the time of its publication was that such a novel, bitter, uncompromising, shocking, gave proof, by its very existence, of what strides might be taken in a free democracy; and its indisputable success, proof that Americans were now able to look full in the face without flinching the dreadful facts. Americans, unhappily, have the most remarkable ability to alchemize all bitter truths into an innocuous but piquant confection and to transform their moral contradictions, or public discussion of such contradictions, into a proud decoration, such as is given for heroism on the field of battle. Such a book, we felt with pride, could never have been written before—which was true. Nor could it be written today. It bears already the aspect of a landmark; for Bigger and his brothers have undergone yet another metamorphosis; they have been accepted in baseball leagues and by colleges hitherto exclusive; and they have made a most favorable appearance on the national screen. We have yet to encounter, nevertheless, a report so indisputably authentic, or one that can begin to challenge this most significant novel.

It is, in a certain American tradition, the story of an unremarkable youth in battle with the force of circumstance; that force of circumstance which plays and which has played so important a part in the national fables of success or failure. In this case the force of circumstance is not poverty merely but color, a circumstance which cannot be overcome, against which the protagonist battles for his life and loses. It is, on the surface, remarkable that this book should have enjoyed among Americans the favor it did enjoy; no more remarkable, however, than that it should have been compared, exuberantly, to [Fyodor] Dostoevsky, though placed a shade below [John] Dos Passos, [Theodore] Dreiser, and [John] Steinbeck; and when the book is examined, its impact does not seem remarkable at all, but becomes, on the contrary, perfectly logical and inevitable.

The Social Struggle

We cannot, to begin with, divorce this book from the specific social climate of that time: it was one of the last of those angry productions, encountered in the late twenties and all through the thirties, dealing with the inequities of the social structure of America. It was published one year before our entry into the last world war—which is to say, very few years after the dissolution of the WPA [Works Progress Administration] and the end of the New Deal [the period of economic relief programs created by President Franklin D. Roosevelt in

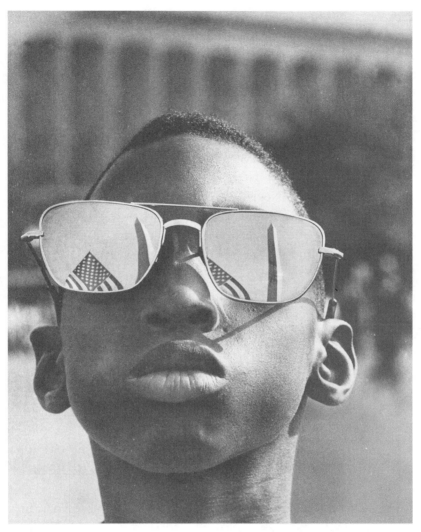

The top of the Washington Monument and part of a U.S. flag are reflected in the sunglasses of a young African American boy as he poses at the Capitol where he joins others in the March on Washington, August 28, 1963. AP Images.

the 1930s] and at a time when bread lines and soup kitchens and bloody industrial battles were bright in everyone's memory. The rigors of that unexpected time filled us not only with a genuinely bewildered and despairing idealism—so that, because there at least was *something* to fight for, young men went off to die in [the civil war in] Spain—but also with a genuinely bewildered self-consciousness. The Negro, who had been during the magnificent twenties a passionate and delightful primitive, now became, as one of the things we were most self-conscious about, our most oppressed minority. In the thirties, swallowing [German philosopher of communism Karl] Marx whole, we discovered the Worker and realized—I should think with some relief—that the aims of the Worker and the aims of the Negro were one. This theorem—to which we shall return—seems now to leave rather too much out of account; it became, nevertheless, one of the slogans of the "class struggle" and the gospel of the New Negro.

As for this New Negro, it was Wright who became his most eloquent spokesman; and his work, from its beginning, is most clearly committed to the social struggle. Leaving aside the considerable question of what relationship precisely the artist bears to the revolutionary, the reality of man as a social being is not his only reality and that artist is strangled who is forced to deal with human beings solely in social terms; and who has, moreover, as Wright had, the necessity thrust on him of being the representative of some thirteen million people. It is a false responsibility (since writers are not congressmen) and impossible, by its nature, of fulfillment. The unlucky shepherd soon finds that, so far from being able to feed the hungry sheep, he has lost the wherewithal for his own nourishment: having not been allowed—so fearful was his burden, so present his audience!—to recreate his own experience. Further, the militant men and women of the thirties were not, upon examination, significantly emancipated from their antecedents, however bitterly they might consider themselves estranged or however gallantly they struggled to build a better world. However they might extol [the Communist system of] Russia, their concept of a better world was quite helplessly American and betrayed a certain thinness of imagination, a suspect reliance on suspect and badly digested formulae, and a positively fretful romantic haste. Finally, the relationship of the Negro to the Worker cannot be summed up, nor even greatly illuminated, by saying that their aims are one. It is true only insofar as they both desire better working conditions and useful only insofar as they unite their strength as workers to achieve these ends. Further than this we cannot in honesty go.

In this climate Wright's voice first was heard and the struggle which promised for a time to shape his work and give it purpose also fixed it in an ever more unrewarding rage. Recording his days of anger he has also nevertheless recorded, as no Negro before him had ever done, that fantasy Americans hold in their minds when they speak of the Negro: that fantastic and fearful image which we have lived with since the first slave fell beneath the lash. This is the significance of *Native Son* and also, unhappily, its overwhelming limitation.

Bigger's Symbolism

Native Son begins with the *Brring!* of an alarm clock in the squalid Chicago tenement where Bigger and his family live. Rats live there too, feeding off the garbage, and we first encounter Bigger in the act of killing one. One may consider that the entire book, from that harsh *Brring!* to Bigger's weak "Good-by" as the lawyer, Max, leaves him in the death cell, is an extension, with the roles inverted, of this chilling metaphor. Bigger's situation and Bigger himself exert on the mind the same sort of fascination. The premise of the book is, as I take it, clearly conveyed in these first pages: we are confronting a monster created by the American republic and we are, through being made to share his experience, to receive illumination as regards the manner of his life and to feel both pity and horror at his awful and inevitable doom. This is an arresting and potentially rich idea and we would be discussing a very different novel if Wright's execution had been more perceptive and if he had not attempted to redeem a symbolical monster in social terms.

One may object that it was precisely Wright's intention to create in Bigger a social symbol, revelatory of social disease and prophetic of disaster. I think, however, that it is this assumption which we ought to examine more carefully. Bigger has no discernible relationship to himself, to his own life, to his own people, nor to any other people—in this respect, perhaps, he is most American—and his force comes, not from his significance as a social (or anti-social) unit, but from his significance as the incarnation of a myth. It is remarkable that, though we follow him step by step from the tenement room to the death cell, we know as little about him when this journey is ended as we did when it began; and, what is even more remarkable, we know almost as little about the social dynamic which we are to believe created him. Despite the details of slum life which we are given, I doubt that anyone who has thought about it, disengaging himself from sentimentality, can accept this most essential premise of the novel for a moment.

Those Negroes who surround him, on the other hand, his hard-working mother, his ambitious sister, his poolroom cronies, Bessie, might be considered as far richer and far more subtle and accurate illustrations of the ways in which Negroes are controlled in our society and the complex techniques they have evolved for their survival. We are limited, however, to Bigger's view of them, part of a deliberate plan which might not have been disastrous if we were not also limited to Bigger's perceptions. What this means for the novel is that a necessary dimension has been cut away; this dimension being the relationship that Negroes bear to one another, that depth of involvement and unspoken recognition of shared experience which creates a way of life. What the novel reflects—and at no point interprets—is the isolation of the Negro within his own group and the resulting fury of impatient scorn. It is this which creates its climate of anarchy and unmotivated and unapprehended disaster; and it is this climate, common to most Negro protest novels, which has led us all to believe that in

Negro life there exists no tradition, no field of manners, no possibility of ritual or intercourse, such as may, for example, sustain the Jew even after he has left his father's house. But the fact is not that the Negro has no tradition but that there has as yet arrived no sensibility sufficiently profound and tough to make this tradition articulate. For a tradition expresses, after all, nothing more than the long and painful experience of a people; it comes out of the battle waged to maintain their integrity or, to put it more simply, out of their struggle to survive. When we speak of the Jewish tradition we are speaking of centuries of exile and persecution, of the strength which endured and the sensibility which discovered in it the high possibility of the moral victory.

Bigger: The True Native Son

This sense of how Negroes live and how they have so long endured is hidden from us in part by the very speed of the Negro's public progress, a progress so heavy with complexity, so bewildering and kaleidoscopic, that he dare not pause to conjecture on the darkness which lies behind him; and by the nature of the American psychology which, in order to apprehend or be made able to accept it, must undergo a metamorphosis so profound as to be literally unthinkable and which there is no doubt we will resist until we are compelled to achieve our own identity by the rigors of a time that has yet to come. Bigger, in the meanwhile, and all his furious kin, serve only to whet the notorious national taste for the sensational and to reinforce all that we now find it necessary to believe. It is not Bigger whom we fear, since his appearance among us makes our victory certain. It is the others, who smile, who go to church, who give no cause for complaint, whom we sometimes consider with amusement, with pity, even with affection—and in whose faces we sometimes surprise the merest arrogant hint of hatred, the faintest, withdrawn, speculative shadow of contempt—who make us uneasy; whom we cajole, threaten, flatter, fear; who to us remain unknown, though we are not (we feel with both relief and hostility and with bottomless confusion) unknown to them. It is out of our reaction to these hewers of wood and drawers of water that our image of Bigger was created.

It is this image, living yet, which we perpetually seek to evade with good works; and this image which makes of all our good works an intolerable mockery. The "nigger," black, benighted, brutal, consumed with hatred as we are consumed with guilt, cannot be thus blotted out. He stands at our shoulders when we give our maid her wages, it is his hand which we fear we are taking when struggling to communicate with the current "intelligent" Negro, his stench, as it were, which fills our mouths with salt as the monument is unveiled in honor of the latest Negro leader. Each generation has shouted behind him, *Nigger!* as he walked our streets; it is he whom we would rather our sisters did not marry; he is banished into the vast and wailing outer darkness whenever we speak of the "purity" of our women, of the "sanctity" of our homes, of "American" ideals. What is more, he knows it. He is indeed the "native son": he is the "nigger." Let us refrain from inquiring at the moment whether or not he actually exists; for we *believe* that he exists. Whenever we encounter him amongst us in the flesh, our faith is made perfect and his necessary and bloody end is executed with a mystical ferocity of joy.

The Cost of Oppression and Submission

Irving Howe

Irving Howe was the founding editor of Dissent *magazine, a City University of New York Distinguished Professor of Literature, a founder of Democratic Socialists of America, a leading literary critic, and author. He died in 1993.*

In his criticism of Native Son, *James Baldwin neglected to acknowledge how the novel served as a model for future African American writers like him writes Irving Howe. While Baldwin's arguments that* Native Son *failed to represent African American traditions and relationships to one another holds weight, Howe believes his other criticisms were too harsh. To Howe,* Native Son *symbolized the experience of Richard Wright, and thus, the experience of the black man of the time.*

James Baldwin first came to the notice of the American literary public not through his own fiction but as author of an impassioned criticism of the conventional Negro novel. In 1949 he published in *Partisan Review* an essay called "Everybody's Protest Novel," attacking the kind of fiction, from *Uncle Tom's Cabin* to *Native Son*, that had been written about the ordeal of the American Negroes; and two years later he printed in the same magazine "Many Thousands Gone," a tougher and more explicit polemic against Richard Wright and the school of naturalistic "protest" fiction that Wright represented. The protest novel, wrote Baldwin, is undertaken out of sympathy for the Negro, but through its need to present him merely as a social victim or a mythic agent of sexual prowess, it hastens to confine the Negro to the very tones of

Irving Howe, "Black Boys and Native Sons," *Dissent*, vol. 10, no. 4, Autumn 1963, pp. 353–368. Copyright © 1963 by the Foundation for the Study of Independent Social Ideas, Inc. Copyright © renewed 1991 by Dissent. Reproduced by permission.

violence he has known all his life. Compulsively reenacting and magnifying his trauma, the protest novel proves unable to transcend it. So choked with rage has this kind of writing become, it cannot show the Negro as a unique person or locate him as a member of a community with its own traditions and values, its own "unspoken recognition of shared experience which creates a way of life." The failure of the protest novel "lies in its insistence that it is [man's] categorization alone which is real and which cannot be transcended."

Like all attacks launched by young writers against their famous elders, Baldwin's essays were also a kind of announcement of his own intentions. He wrote admiringly about Wright's courage ("his work was an immense liberation and revelation for me"), but now, precisely because Wright had prepared the way for all the Negro writers to come, he, Baldwin, would go further, transcending the sterile categories of "Negro-ness," whether those enforced by the white world or those defensively erected by the Negroes themselves. No longer mere victim or rebel, the Negro would stand free in a self-achieved humanity. As Baldwin put it some years later, he hoped "to prevent myself from becoming *merely* a Negro; or even, merely a Negro writer." The world "tends to trap and immobilize you in the role you play," and for the Negro writer, if he is to be a writer at all, it hardly matters whether the trap is sprung from motives of hatred or condescension.

Sociology of Existence

Baldwin's rebellion against the older Negro novelist who had served him as a model and had helped launch his career, was not of course an unprecedented event. The history of literature is full of such painful ruptures, and the issue Baldwin raised is one that keeps recurring, usually as an aftermath to a period of "socially engaged" writing. The novel is an inherently ambiguous genre: it strains toward formal autonomy and can seldom avoid being a public gesture. If it is true, as

Baldwin said in "Everybody's Protest Novel," that "literature and sociology are not one and the same," it is equally true that such statements hardly begin to cope with the problem of how a writer's own experience affects his desire to represent human affairs in a work of fiction. Baldwin's formula evades, through rhetorical sweep, the genuinely difficult issue of the relationship between social experience and literature.

Yet in *Notes of a Native Son*, the book in which his remark appears, Baldwin could also say: "One writes out of one thing only one's own experience." What, then, was the experience of a man with a black skin, what *could* it be in this country? How could a Negro put pen to paper, how could he so much as think or breathe, without some impulsion to protest, be it harsh or mild, political or private, released or buried? The "sociology" of his existence formed a constant pressure on his literary work, and not merely in the way this might be true for any writer, but with a pain and ferocity that nothing could remove

James Baldwin's early essays are superbly eloquent, displaying virtually in full the gifts that would enable him to become one of the great American rhetoricians. But these essays, like some of the later ones, are marred by rifts in logic, so little noticed when one gets swept away by the brilliance of the language that it takes a special effort to attend their argument.

Later Baldwin would see the problems of the Negro writer with a greater charity and more mature doubt. Reviewing in 1959 a book of poems by Langston Hughes, he wrote: "Hughes is an American Negro poet and has no choice but to be acutely aware of it. He is not the first American Negro to find the war between his social and artistic responsibilities all but irreconcilable." All but irreconcilable: the phrase strikes a note sharply different from Baldwin's attack upon Wright in the early fifties. And it is not hard to surmise the reasons for this change. In the intervening years Baldwin had been living through some of the experiences that had goaded Richard Wright into rage and driven him into exile; he too, like Wright, had been to hell and back, many times over.

What Wright Had Begun

The day *Native Son* appeared, American culture was changed forever. No matter how much qualifying the book might later need, it made impossible a repetition of the old lies. In all its crudeness, melodrama and claustrophobia of vision, Richard Wright's novel brought out into the open, as no one ever had before, the hatred, fear and violence that have crippled and may yet destroy our culture.

A blow at the white man, the novel forced him to recognize himself as an oppressor. A blow at the black man, the novel forced him to recognize the cost of his submission. *Native Son* assaulted the most cherished of American vanities: the hope that the accumulated injustice of the past would bring with it no lasting penalties, the fantasy that in his humiliation the Negro somehow retained a sexual potency—or was it a childlike good-nature?—that made it necessary to envy and still more to suppress him. Speaking from the black wrath of retribution, Wright insisted that history can be a punishment. He told us the one thing even the most liberal whites preferred not to hear: that Negroes were far from patient or forgiving, that they were scarred by fear, that they hated every moment of their suppression even when seeming most acquiescent, and that often enough they hated us, the decent and cultivated white men who from complicity or neglect shared in the responsibility for their plight. If such younger novelists as Baldwin and Ralph Ellison were to move beyond Wright's harsh naturalism and toward more supple modes of fiction, that was possible only because Wright had been there first, courageous enough to release the full weight of his anger.

African American men rounded up after wartime riots between blacks and whites that re-quired the use of Army troops and martial law, Michigan, June 20, 1943. Gordon Coster/ Time & Life Pictures/Getty Images.

Bigger Thomas Part of Many

In *Black Boy*, the autobiographical narrative he published sev-eral years later, Wright would tell of an experience he had while working as a bellboy in the South. Many times he had come into a hotel room carrying luggage or food and seen na-ked white women lounging about, unmoved by shame at his presence, for "blacks were not considered human being anyway. . . . I was a non-man. . . . I felt doubly cast out." With the publication of *Native Son*, however, Wright forced his readers to acknowledge his anger, and in that way, if none other, he wrested for himself a sense of dignity as a man. He forced his readers to confront the disease of our culture, and to one of its most terrifying symptoms he gave the name of Bigger Thomas.

Brutal and brutalized, lost forever to his unexpended hatred and his fear of the world, a numbed and illiterate black boy stumbling into a murder and never, not even at the edge of the electric chair, breaking through to an understanding of either his plight or himself, Bigger Thomas was a part of Richard Wright, a part even of the James Baldwin who stared with horror at Wright's Bigger, unable either to absorb him into his consciousness or eject him from it. Enormous courage, a discipline of self-conquest, was required to conceive Bigger Thomas, for this was no eloquent Negro spokesman, no admirable intellectual or formidable proletarian. Bigger was drawn—one would surmise, deliberately—from white fantasy and white contempt. Bigger was the worst of Negro life accepted, then rendered a trifle conscious and thrown back at those who had made him what he was. "No American Negro exists," Baldwin would later write, "who does not have his private Bigger Thomas living in the skull."

Battling a Great Natural Force

Wright drove his narrative to the very core of American phobia: sexual fright, sexual violation. He understood that the fantasy of rape is a consequence of guilt, what the whites suppose themselves to deserve. He understood that the white man's notion of uncontaminated Negro vitality, little as it had to do with the bitter realities of Negro life, reflected some ill-formed and buried feeling that our culture has run down, lost its blood, become febrile. And he grasped the way in which the sexual issue has been intertwined with social relationships, for even as the white people who hire Bigger as their chauffeur are decent and charitable, even as the girl he accidentally kills is a liberal of sorts, theirs is the power and the privilege. "We black and they white. They got things and we ain't. They do things and we can't."

The novel barely stops to provision a recognizable social world, often contenting itself with cartoon simplicities and yielding almost entirely to the nightmare incomprehension of Bigger Thomas. The mood is apocalyptic, the tone superbly aggressive. Wright was an existentialist long before he heard the name, for he was committed to the literature of extreme situations both through the pressures of his rage and the gasping hope of an ultimate catharsis.

Wright confronts both the violence and the crippling limitations of Bigger Thomas. For Bigger white people are not people at all, but something more, "a sort of great natural force, like a stormy sky looming overhead." And only through violence does he gather a little meaning in life, pitifully little: "he had murdered and created a new life for himself." Beyond that Bigger cannot go.

A Work of Assault

At first *Native Son* seems still another naturalistic novel: a novel of exposure and accumulation, charting the waste of the undersides of the American city. Behind the book one senses the molding influence of [American novelist] Theodore Dreiser, especially the Dreiser of *An American Tragedy* who knows there are situations so oppressive that only violence can provide their victims with the hope of dignity. Like Dreiser, Wright wished to pummel his readers into awareness; like Dreiser, to overpower them with the sense of society as an enclosing force. Yet the comparison is finally of limited value, and for the disconcerting reason that Dreiser had a white skin and Wright a black one.

The usual naturalistic novel is written with detachment, as if by a scientist surveying a field of operations; it is a novel in which the writer withdraws from a detested world and coldly piles up the evidence for detesting it. *Native Son*, though preserving some of the devices of the naturalistic novel, deviates sharply from its characteristic tone: a tone Wright could not possibly have maintained and which, it may be, no Negro novelist can really hold for long. *Native Son* is a work of assault rather than withdrawal; the author yields himself in part to a vision of nightmare. Bigger's cowering perception of the world becomes the most vivid and authentic component of the book. Naturalism pushed to an extreme turns here into something other than itself, a kind of expressionist outburst, no longer a replica of the familiar social world but a self-contained realm of grotesque emblems. . . .

Rage and Liberation

The reality pressing upon all of Wright's work was a nightmare of remembrance, everything from which he had pulled himself out, with an effort and at a cost that is almost unimaginable. Without the terror of that nightmare it would have been impossible for Wright to summon the truth of the reality—not the only truth about American Negroes, perhaps not even the deepest one, but a primary and inescapable truth. Both truth and terror rested on a gross fact which Wright alone dared to confront: that violence is central to the life of the American Negro, defining and crippling him with a harshness few other Americans need suffer. "No American Negro exists who does not have his private Bigger Thomas living in the skull."

Now I think it would be well not to judge in the abstract, or with much haste, the violence that gathers in the Negro's heart as a response to the violence he encounters in society. It would be well to see this violence as part of an historical experience that is open to moral scrutiny but ought to be shielded from presumptuous moralizing. Bigger Thomas may be enslaved to a hunger for violence, but anyone reading *Native Son* with mere courtesy must observe the way in which Wright, even while yielding emotionally to Bigger's deprivation, also struggles to transcend it. That he did not fully succeed seems obvious; one may doubt that any Negro writer could.

More subtle and human than Baldwin's criticism is a remark made some years ago by Isaac Rosenfeld while reviewing
Black Boy: "As with all Negroes and all men who are born to
suffer social injustice, part of [Wright's] humanity found itself
only in acquaintance with violence, and in hatred of the oppressor." Surely Rosenfeld was not here inviting an easy acqui-
escence in violence; he was trying to suggest the historical
context, the psychological dynamics, which condition the attitudes all Negro writers take, or must take, toward violence. To
say this is not to propose the condescension of exempting Negro writers from moral judgment, but to suggest the terms of
understanding, and still more, the terms of hesitation for
making a judgment.

There were times when Baldwin grasped this point better
than anyone else. If he could speak of the "unrewarding rage"
of *Native Son*, he also spoke of the book as "an immense liberation." Is it impudent to suggest that one reason he felt the
book to be a liberation was precisely its rage, precisely the relief and pleasure that he, like so many other Negroes, must
have felt upon seeing those long-suppressed emotions finally
breaking through?. . .

Humanity Only Through Struggle

If Bigger Thomas, as Baldwin said, "accepted a theology that
denies him life," if in his Negro self-hatred he "*wants* to die
because he glories in his hatred," this did not constitute a
criticism of Wright unless one were prepared to assume what
was simply preposterous: that Wright, for all his emotional involvement with Bigger, could not see beyond the limitations
of the character he had created. This was a question Baldwin
never seriously confronted in his early essays. He would describe accurately the limitations of Bigger Thomas and then,
by one of those rhetorical leaps at which he is so gifted, would
assume that these were also the limitations of Wright or his
book.

Still another ground for Baldwin's attack was his reluctance to accept the clenched militancy of Wright's posture as both novelist and man. In a remarkable sentence appearing in "Everybody's Protest Novel" Baldwin wrote: "our humanity is our burden, our life; we need not battle for it; we need only to do what is infinitely more difficult—that is, accept it." What Baldwin was saying here was part of the outlook so many American intellectuals took over during the years of a postwar liberalism not very different from conservatism. Ralph Ellison expressed this view in terms still more extreme: "Thus to see America with an awareness of its rich diversity and its almost magical fluidity and freedom, I was forced to conceive of a novel unburdened by the narrow naturalism which has led after so many triumphs to the final and unrelieved despair which marks so much of our current fiction." This note of willed affirmation was to be heard in many other works of the early fifties, most notably in Saul Bellow's *Adventures of Augie March*. Today it is likely to strike one as a note whistled in the dark In response to Baldwin and Ellison, Wright would have said (I virtually quote the words he used in talking to me during the summer of 1958) that only through struggle could men with black skins, and for that matter, all the oppressed of the world, achieve their humanity. It was a lesson, said Wright with a touch of bitterness yet not without kindness, that the younger writers would have to learn in their own way and their own time. All that has happened since, bears him out.

Where Is the Tradition?

One criticism made by Baldwin in writing about *Native Son*, perhaps because it is the least ideological, remains important. He complained that in Wright's novel "a necessary dimension has been cut away; this dimension being the relationship that Negroes bear to one another, that depth of involvement and unspoken recognition of shared experience which creates a way of life." The climate of the book, "common to most Negro protest novels ... has led us all to believe that in Negro life there exists no tradition, no field of manners, no possibility of ritual or intercourse, such as may, for example, sustain the Jew even after he has left his father's house." It could be urged, perhaps, that in composing a novel verging on expressionism Wright need not be expected to present the Negro world with fullness, balance or nuance; but there can be little doubt that in this respect Baldwin did score a major point: the posture of militancy, no matter how great the need for it, exacts a heavy price from the writer, as indeed from everyone else. For "Even the hatred of squalor/Makes the brow grow stern/Even anger against injustice/Makes the voice grow harsh. . . ." All one can ask, by way of reply, is whether the refusal to struggle may not exact a still greater price. It is a question that would soon be tormenting James Baldwin, and almost against his will.

Black Life No Mere Abstraction

Ralph Ellison

Ralph Ellison was an African American writer best known for his novel Invisible Man. *He was also a jazz trumpeter and a photographer. Ellison died in 1994.*

Ralph Ellison argues that there has been no single shared experience of the black man, as he perceived Irving Howe to be promoting in Howe's critique of Native Son. *Instead, Ellison believes that as much as color, and society's reaction to it, shapes the black man, so does that man's individual experience and free will. Through his own free will, he is able to free himself through art, not through what Ellison calls propaganda. In Ellison's eyes, literature should first and foremost be literature, a piece of art, not political propaganda, as he views* Native Son *to be.*

One unfamiliar with what [Irving] Howe stands for would get the impression that when he looks at a Negro he sees not a human being but an abstract embodiment of living hell. He seems never to have considered that American Negro life (and here he is encouraged by certain Negro "spokesmen") is, for the Negro who must live it, not only a burden (and not always that) but also a *discipline*—just as any human life which has endured so long is a discipline teaching its own insights into the human condition, its own strategies of survival. There is a fullness, even a richness here; and here *despite* the realities of politics, perhaps, but nevertheless here and real. Because it is *human* life. And Wright, for all of his indictments, was no less its product than that other talented Mississippian, [black American operatic diva] Leontyne Price. To deny in the interest of revolutionary posture that such possibilities of human

Ralph Ellison, *Shadow and Act*. New York: Random House, 1964, pp. 107–43.

richness exist for others, even in Mississippi, is not only to deny us our humanity but to betray the critic's commitment to social reality. Critics who do so should abandon literature for politics.

For even as his life toughens the Negro, even as it brutalizes him, sensitizes him, dulls him, goads him to anger, moves him to irony, sometimes fracturing and sometimes affirming his hopes; even as it shapes his attitudes toward family, sex, love, religion; even as it modulates his humor, tempers his joy—it *conditions* him to deal with his life and with himself. Because it is *his* life and no mere abstraction in someone's head. He must live it and try consciously to grasp its complexity until he can change it; must live it *as* he changes it. He is no mere product of his socio-political predicament. He is a product of the interaction between his racial predicament, his individual will and the broader American cultural freedom in which he finds his ambiguous existence. Thus he, too, in a limited way, is his own creation.

Struggle and Humanity

In his loyalty to Richard Wright, Howe considers Ellison and Baldwin guilty of filial betrayal because, in their own work, they have rejected the path laid down by *Native Son*, phonies because, while actually "black boys," they pretend to be mere American writers trying to react to something of the pluralism of their predicament.

In his myth Howe takes the roles of both Shem and Japheth[1] trying mightily (his face turned backward so as not to see what it is he's veiling) to cover the old man's bare belly, and then becoming Wright's voice from beyond the grave by uttering the curses which Wright was too ironic or too proud to have uttered himself, at least in print:

1. The reference is to Genesis 9:20–27, the story of two sons of Noah who out of respect covered up their father's naked body as he lay passed out in his tent. In contrast, their brother Ham looked upon his father's nakedness and was cursed.

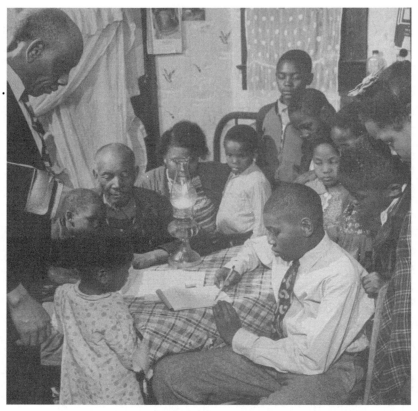

An African American family in the Memphis area gathered around a kitchen table. Wright also spent time in Memphis, where he began another one of his novels, Black Boy. Ed Clark/Time & Life Pictures/Getty Images.

In response to Baldwin and Ellison, Wright would have said (I virtually quote the words he used in talking to me during the summer of 1958) that only through struggle could men with black skins, and for that matter, all the oppressed of the world, achieve their humility [Howe used the word "humanity"]. It was a lesson, said Wright, with a touch of bitterness yet not without kindness, that the younger writers would have to learn in their own way and their own time. All that has happened since bears him out.

What, coming eighteen years after *Native Son* and thirteen years after World War II, does this rather limp cliché mean?

Nor is it clear what is meant by the last sentence—or is it that today Baldwin has come to out-Wrighting Richard? The real questions seem to be: How does the Negro writer participate *as a writer* in the struggle for human freedom? To whom does he address his work? What values emerging from Negro experience does he try to affirm?

I started with the primary assumption that men with black skins, having retained their humanity before all of the conscious efforts made to dehumanize them, especially following the Reconstruction [the period following the Civil War, when the U.S. government tried to "reconstruct" the South], are unquestionably human. Thus they have the obligation of freeing themselves—whoever their allies might be—by depending upon the validity of their own experience for an accurate picture of the reality which they seek to change, and for a gauge of the values they would see made manifest. Crucial to this view is the belief that their resistance to provocation, their coolness under pressure, their sense of timing and their tenacious hold on the ideal of their ultimate freedom are indispensable values in the struggle, and are at least as characteristic of American Negroes as the hatred, fear and vindictiveness which Wright chose to emphasize.

Novels as Weapons

Wright believed in the much abused idea that novels are "weapons"—the counterpart of the dreary notion, common among most minority groups, that novels are instruments of good public relations. But I believe that true novels, even when most pessimistic and bitter, arise out of an impulse to celebrate human life and therefore are ritualistic and ceremonial at their core. Thus they would preserve as they destroy, affirm as they reject.

In *Native Son*, Wright began with the ideological proposition that what whites think of the Negro's reality is more important than what Negroes themselves know it to be. Hence

Bigger Thomas was presented as a near-subhuman indictment of white oppression. He was designed to shock whites out of their apathy and end the circumstances out of which Wright insisted Bigger emerged. Here environment is all—and interestingly enough, environment conceived solely in terms of the physical, the non-conscious. Well, cut off my legs and call me Shorty! Kill my parents and throw me on the mercy of the court as an orphan! Wright could imagine Bigger, but Bigger could not possibly imagine Richard Wright. Wright saw to that.

But without arguing Wright's right to his personal vision, I would say that he was himself a better argument for my approach than Bigger was for his. And so, to be fair and as inclusive as Howe, is James Baldwin. Both are true Negro Americans, and both affirm the broad possibility of personal realization which I see as a saving aspect of American life. Surely, this much can be admitted without denying the injustice which all three of us have protested.

Howe is impressed by Wright's pioneering role and by the "... enormous courage, the discipline of self-conquest required to conceive Bigger Thomas...." And earlier: "If such younger novelists as Baldwin and Ralph Ellison were able to move beyond Wright's harsh naturalism toward more supple modes of fiction, that was only possible because Wright had been there first, courageous enough to release the full weight of his anger."

It is not for me to judge Wright's courage, but I must ask just why it was possible for me to write as I write "only" because Wright released his anger? Can't I be allowed to release my own? What does Howe know of my acquaintance with violence, or the shape of my courage or the intensity of my anger? I suggest that my credentials are at least as valid as Wright's, even though he began writing long before I did, and it is possible that I have lived through and committed even more violence than he. Howe must wait for an autobiography before he can be responsibly certain. Everybody wants to tell us what a Negro is, yet few wish, even in a joke, to be one. But if you would tell me who I am, at least take the trouble to discover what I have been.

Freedom Through Individual Aspiration

Which brings me to the most distressing aspect of Howe's thinking: his Northern white liberal version of the white Southern myth of absolute separation of the races. He implies that Negroes can only aspire to contest other Negroes, and must wait for the appearance of a Black Hope before they have the courage to move. Howe is so committed to a socio-logical vision of society that he apparently cannot see (perhaps because he is dealing with Negroes—although not because he would suppress us socially or politically, for in fact he is anxious to end such suppression) that whatever the efficiency of segregation as a socio-political arrangement, it has been far from absolute on the level of *culture*. Southern whites cannot walk, talk, sing, conceive of laws or justice, think of sex, love, the family or freedom without responding to the presence of Negroes.

Similarly, no matter how strictly Negroes are segregated socially and politically, on the level of the imagination their ability to achieve freedom is limited only by their individual aspiration, insight, energy and will. Wright was able to free himself in Mississippi because he had the imagination and the will to do so. He was as much a product of his reading as of his painful experiences, and he made himself a writer by subjecting himself to the writer's discipline—as he understood it. The same is true of James Baldwin, who is not the product of a Negro store-front church but of the library, and the same is true of me.

Freedom Through Art and Self

Howe seems to see segregation as an opaque steel jug with the Negroes inside waiting for some black messiah to come along and blow the cork. Wright is his hero and he sticks with him loyally. But if we are in a jug it is transparent, not opaque, and one is allowed not only to see outside but to read what is going on out there; to make identifications as to values and human quality. So in Macon County, Alabama, I read [Karl] Marx, [Sigmund] Freud, T.S. Eliot, [Ezra] Pound, Gertrude Stein and [Ernest] Hemingway. Books which seldom, if ever, mentioned Negroes were to release me from whatever "segregated" idea I might have had of my human possibilities. I was freed not by propagandists or by the example of Wright—I did not know him at the time and was earnestly trying to learn enough to write a symphony and have it performed by the time I was twenty-six, because [Richard] Wagner had done so and I admired his music—but by composers, novelists, and poets who spoke to me of more interesting and freer ways of life.

These were works which, by fulfilling themselves as works of art, by being satisfied to deal with life in terms of their own sources of power, were able to give me a broader sense of life and possibility. Indeed, I understand a bit more about myself as Negro because literature has taught me something of my identity as Western man, as political being. It has also taught me something of the cost of being an individual who aspires to conscious eloquence. It requires real poverty of the imagination to think that this can come to a Negro *only* through the example of *other Negroes*, especially after the performance of the slaves in re-creating themselves, in good part, out of the images and myths of the Old Testament Jews. . . .

The Authentic Tone

While I rejected Bigger Thomas as any *final* image of Negro personality, I recognized *Native Son* as an achievement; as one man's essay in defining the human condition as seen from a specific Negro perspective at a given time in a given place. And I was proud to have known Wright and happy for the impact he had made upon our apathy. But Howe's ideas notwithstanding, history is history, cultural contacts ever mysterious, and taste exasperatingly personal. Two days after arriving in New York I was to read [André] Malraux's *Man's Fate* and *The Days of Wrath*, and after these how could I be impressed by Wright as an ideological novelist? Need my skin blind me to all other values? Yet Howe writes:

> When Negro liberals write that despite the prevalence of bias there has been an improvement in the life of their people, such statements are reasonable and necessary. But what have these to do with the way Negroes feel, with the power of the memories they must surely retain? About this we know very little and would be well advised not to nourish preconceptions, for their feelings may well be closer to Wright's rasping outbursts than to the more modulated tones of the younger Negro novelists. *Wright remembered*, and what he remembered other Negroes must also have remembered. And in that way he kept faith with the experience of the boy who had fought his way out of the depths, to speak for those who remained there.

Wright, for Howe, is the genuine article, the authentic Negro writer, and his tone the only authentic tone. But why strip Wright of his individuality in order to criticize other writers? He had his memories and I have mine, just as I suppose Irving Howe has his—or has Marx spoken the final word for him? Indeed, very early in *Black Boy*, Wright's memory and his contact with literature come together in a way revealing, at least to the eye concerned with Wright the literary man, that his manner of keeping faith with the Negroes who remained in the depths is quite interesting:

> (After I had outlived the shocks of childhood, after the habit of reflection had been born in me, I used to mull over the strange absence of real kindness in Negroes, how unstable was our tenderness, how lacking in genuine passion we were, how void of great hope, how timid our joy, how bare our

traditions, how hollow our memories, how lacking we were in those intangible sentiments that bind man to man and how shallow was even our despair. After I had learned other ways of life I used to brood upon the unconscious irony of those who felt that Negroes led so passional an existence! I saw that what had been taken for our emotional strength was our negative confusions, our flights, our fears, our frenzy under pressure.

(Whenever I thought of the essential bleakness of black life in America, I knew that Negroes had never been allowed to catch the full spirit of Western civilization, that they lived somehow in it but not of it. And when I brooded upon the cultural barrenness of black life, I wondered if clean, positive tenderness, love, honor, loyalty and the capacity to remember were native with man. I asked myself if these human qualities were not fostered, won, struggled and suffered for, preserved in ritual from one generation to another.)

Defining Humanity

Must I be condemned because my sense of Negro life was quite different? Or because for me keeping faith would never allow me to even raise such a question about any segment of humanity? *Black Boy* is not a sociological case history but an autobiography, and therefore a work of art shaped by a writer bent upon making an ideological point. Doubtlessly, this was the beginning of Wright's exile, the making of a decision which was to shape his life and writing thereafter. And it is precisely at this point that Wright is being what I would call, in Howe's words, "literary to a fault."

For just as *How Bigger Was Born* is Wright's Jamesian preface to *Native Son*, the passage quoted above is his paraphrase of Henry James' catalogue of those items of a high civilization which were absent from American life during [Nathaniel] Hawthorne's day, and which seemed so necessary in order for the novelist to function. This, then, was Wright's list of those items of high humanity which he found missing among Negroes. Thank God, I have never been quite that literary.

How awful that Wright found the facile answers of Marxism before he learned to use literature as a means for discovering the forms of American Negro humanity. I could not and cannot question their existence, I can only seek again and again to project that humanity as I see it and feel it. To me Wright as *writer* was less interesting than the enigma he personified: that he could so dissociate himself from the complexity of his background while trying so hard to improve the condition of black men everywhere; that he could be so wonderful an example of human possibility but could not for ideological reasons depict a Negro as intelligent, as creative or as dedicated as himself.

In his effort to resuscitate Wright, Irving Howe would designate the role which Negro writers are to play more rigidly than any Southern politician—and for the best of reasons. We must express "black" anger and "clenched militancy"; most of all we should not become too interested in the problems of the art of literature, even though it is through these that we seek our individual identities. And between writing well and being ideologically militant, we must choose militancy.

Well, it all sounds quite familiar and I fear the social order which it forecasts more than I do that of Mississippi. Ironically, during the 1940s it was one of the main sources of Wright's rage and frustration.

Social Critiques of *Native Son* Anger Wright

Addison Gayle

Addison Gayle was a literary critic, essayist, biographer, educator, and lecturer who published The Black Aesthetic *in 1971. Gayle died in 1991.*

After Native Son *was published, reactionary white critics lambasted the novel, claiming that it was impossible for a country to be without racial prejudices. In response, Richard Wright offered Mexico as an example of such a possibility, as a place where people of different ethnic identities did not discriminate against one another. But Addison Gayle notes that more difficult for Wright was to read the criticism from fellow Communists who believed Bigger Thomas was a terrible representation of the black man in America. To this, Wright argued that, even for the sake of the Communist Party, he could not abandon the Bigger Thomases in the country.*

Native Son *was published on March 1, 1940, and was an instantaneous success. The first novel by a black writer to be so chosen, it became a Book-of-the-Month Club selection. In three weeks, the novel sold over a quarter of a million copies. Magazines pursued the author for biographical sketches and interviews. Radio talk shows and lecture rostrums beckoned. His name was added to "The Wall of Fame" at the re-opening of the New York World's Fair and letters poured in from across the country, many congratulatory, some venomous. Book reviews were, on the whole, filled with praise. . . .

The review by David L. Cohn was one of two that provoked Wright's angriest reaction. "Justice or no justice," Cohn

Addison Gayle, *Richard Wright: Ordeal of a Native Son.* New York: Anchor Press/Doubleday, 1980. Copyright © 1980 by Addison Gayle. Used by permission of Marie Brown Associates.

concluded his article, "the whites of America simply will not grant to Negroes at this time those things that Mr. Wright demands. The Negro problem in America is actually insoluble. . . . Hatred, and the preaching of hatred, and incitement to violence can only make a tolerable relationship intolerable." By June 1940, when Wright's reply, "I Bite the Hand That Feeds Me," appeared in the same magazine as Cohn's article, he was in Cuernavaca, Mexico. "The Negro problem in America is not," he wrote, "beyond solution. (I write from a country—Mexico—where people of all races and colors live in harmony and without racial prejudices or theories of racial superiority. Whites and Indians live and work and die here, always resisting the attempts of Anglo-Saxon tourists and industrialists to introduce racial hate and discrimination . . .) at no time in the history of American politics has a Negro stood for anything but the untrammeled rights of human personality, *his* and *others*."

Waiting for Party Appraisal

Such criticism as Cohn's, and Burton Rascoe's, which appeared in the *American Mercury* in May [1940], was irritating but hardly devastating. Reactionary whites of course would have strong personal reactions to his novel. But the critical appraisals he waited for were from the [Communist] Party. In the interests of personal and emotional truth, he had, he knew, committed several "indiscretions" that would offend the more parochial Communists. "He really wanted the Party to like that book," remarked a friend; "I thought he paid too much attention to what they would say. But he was concerned." "Dick told me," [American journalist and politician] Horace Cayton remarked later, "about the Party's reaction to *Native Son*. Since the book did not follow the orthodox Marxist line on the Negro question, the Communists were quite hostile. . . ." The hostility, like the criticism, was slow in coming. [Communists] Mike Gold and Samuel Sillen were complimentary in their appraisals of the book. Still, the review that he waited for most desperately was from the black leadership of the Party. A favorable word from [James] Ford [the most prominent black Communist in the U.S. during the 1930s and early 1940s] or Ben Davis [black Communist who was elected to the New York City council in 1943] would still all party criticism. Ford, however, might not acquiesce, as he was intractable. He had risen in the party ranks because of his skill at political compromise. Party law, for him, was doctrine. But Davis was different. He was an intellectual; he had lived in both worlds, that of the bourgeois blacks and that of the urban proletariat. He walked the streets of Harlem daily, was well known and respected among workers and the bourgeois alike. Certainly, he would recognize the truth and reality of Bigger Thomas. In April, writing in the New York Sunday *Worker*, Davis gave his long-awaited critical appraisal of *Native Son*.

He called the book an important achievement, "the most powerful and important novel of 1940." The writer's objectives, he thought, demanded congratulations: he wanted to demonstrate the degrading and oppressive nature of capitalism; to show that "the Communist Party is the only organization . . . interested in relieving the terrible plight of the Negro people." Yet, the book fell far short of its goal. ". . . every single Negro character," Davis wrote, sounding more now like a black man than a Marxist, "including Bigger's own family is pretty much beaten and desperate. . . . This is where the book falls into one of its most serious errors. Bigger is exaggerated into a symbol of the whole Negro people. . . ." Yet Bigger had little viability as metaphor for American blacks, his reaction to oppression not being that of the vast majority. There were other errors in the book, the depiction of members of the Party, . . . but the portrait of Bigger affronts the Marxist intellectual most of all: ". . . because no other character in the book portrays the Negro masses, the tendency becomes that the reader sees Bigger and no distinction whatever between him and the masses. . . ."

"Politically Naïve"

It was a terrible indictment, striking as severely at the writer's perception of black life in America as at his indiscretions regarding Marxist aesthetic canons. When Mike Gold wrote a favorable review of the book in the *Daily Worker* of April 29, 1940, the Marxist chief's efforts did not calm the angry author: "If I should follow Ben Davis' advice and write of Negroes through the lens of how the Party views them in terms of political theory," he wrote in a letter to Gold, "I'd abandon the Bigger Thomases. I'd be tacitly admitting that they are lost to us, that fascism will triumph because it alone can enlist the allegiance of those millions whom capitalism has crushed and maimed." Nor did personal intervention by Earl Browder in an attempt to somewhat placate this now even more valuable member of the Party assuage his anger: "Earl Browder, head of the American Communist Party, stated that he saw nothing wrong with *Native Son*," said Cayton, "but Dick did not accept this implied invitation to resume his activities in the Party." Still, he was no less committed to the aims of communism than before: "What does fasten my attention upon Communist action," he wrote at a time when party manipulations concerning Hitler and blacks were forcing others from its ranks, "is whether it overcomes settled and ready-made reality, whether it effectively pushes outward and extends the area of human feelings . . . (sometimes I find myself most deeply attracted to it when most people are repelled—that is, for instance, when the U.S.S.R. signed the pact with Nazi Germany). . . ."

This sentiment, expressed in an unpublished essay found among his private papers, demonstrates the validity of [a] later charge, that Wright was "politically naïve." His letter to Mike Gold probably reinforced this conception among other high-ranking Communists like Davis. "It is still possible for a wave of nationalism to sweep the Negro people today," he warned. But, due to an important shift on "the Negro question," occasioned by the Pact, signed in August of 1939, the Party was now fully supporting the old separate-development program for blacks, a program in which nationalism was an accepted reality. In his review of *Native Son*, Davis skillfully forwarded the once discarded thesis: "There is little," Davis criticized *Native Son*, "that directly shows the power of the Negro people, although the book as a whole assumes the existence of the Negro masses. Yet that power is historically present and is evident today in political struggle . . . the failure of the book to bring forward clearly the psychology of the Negro masses will find the capitalist . . . trying to attribute Bigger's attitude to the whole Negro people."

Losing Self-Control

Joseph T. Skerrett Jr.

Joseph T. Skerrett Jr. is a professor of English at the University of Massachusetts–Amherst.

Bigger was a black man trapped in a world of prejudice and discrimination. But Joseph T. Skerrett Jr. notes that instead of embracing religion (like his mother) or alcohol (like Bessie), Bigger found his escape and power through the act of murder. At the end of Native Son, *as Bigger awaited his execution, he saw the purpose in his killing, knowing that his living environment gave him motive for his acts. And regardless of what he had done, Bigger Thomas was a human being.*

Bigger Thomas's situation ... is an imaginative replication of Wright's own "situation." Trapped by the economics of the Depression and the resultant intensification of racial prejudice and discrimination, Bigger feels resentment against the demands of his family—his religious mother, his sister Vera, and his younger brother, Buddy—whose needs require that he submit to the near-slavery of the employment offered by the welfare relief program. Bigger struggles against the family strategies to control his actions without access to the violence that is characteristic of his behavior later in the story. His central counter-strategy is to numb himself to the family feeling within:

> He shut their voices out of his mind. He hated his family because he knew that they were suffering and that he was powerless to help them. He knew that the moment he allowed himself to feel to its fullness how they lived, the shame

Joseph T. Skerrett Jr., *Richard Wright's* Native Son. New York: Chelsea House, 1988. Edited by Harold Bloom. Copyright © 1988 Joseph T. Skerrett, Jr. Reproduced by permission of the author.

and misery of their lives, he would be swept out of himself with fear and despair. So he held toward them an attitude of iron reserve; he lived with them, but behind a wall, a curtain.

(*Native Son*)

This denial is, of course, not without its cost. Bigger must repress his own impulses even more stringently. "He knew that the moment he allowed what his life meant to enter fully into his consciousness, he would either kill himself or someone else. So he denied himself and acted tough.". . .

Bigger's Search for Identity

The fear of the whites threatens Bigger's sense of manly self-control. Amongst the gang it is that fear which creates a brutal community. Bigger humiliates Gus, forcing him to lick the tip of Bigger's knife, in order to prevent the gang from carrying out the planned armed robbery of Blum's. He knew that "the fear of robbing a white man had had a hold of him when he started the fight with Gus." But, as this is a knowledge too costly to be admitted, Bigger's psyche represses it. "He knew it in a way that kept it from coming to his mind in the form of a hard and sharp idea. . . . But he kept this knowledge of his thrust firmly down in him: his courage to live depended upon how successfully his fear was hidden from his consciousness."

This attitude on Bigger's part, this holding his own consciousness at arm's length, is perhaps Wright's most original achievement in his characterization of Bigger. Unlike his creator, Bigger has, as his story opens, almost no access to his own symbolic imagination, his own creative consciousness. His almost formalized imaginative act is the role-playing game he engages Gus in—"playing white." The roles—general, banker, President—are satiric (and thus aggressive) but they are quickly abandoned when their nasty double edge is felt: the absurd pomposity and venality of the powerful whites control the boys' imaginations even in parody. Bigger has never experienced the fulfillment Wright got from the act of writing, that Jamesian [characteristic of author Henry James] sense of an invigorating self-integration and self-satisfaction that is the hallmark of a stable identity. In [literary critic] Francis Fergusson's terminology, the central "action" of the novel, dictated by Bigger's "purpose" in this story, is "to discover an identity." The search for the murderer that occupies the Daltons, the police, and the reporters, the search for motives and evidence by the attorneys, the search for a mode of acquittal by Max are all counterpointed with Bigger's increasingly conscious search for an integrated and satisfying consciousness of who he is.

Bigger's Point of View

This important aspect of Wright's exclusive use of Bigger's point of view has been at the center of the critical contention surrounding the novel's achievement. Some, like [British critic] John Bayliss, see Bigger as merely pathetic in his struggles with consciousness, slow-witted and environmentally unsuited for urban society. More astute critics characteristically lose track of the fact that it is Bigger's point of view we are dealing with, and begin to attribute what Fergusson would call "the movement of the spirit" in the novel entirely to the author's, and not the character's, psyche. Thus [critic] Robert Bone notes that Wright succeeds in balancing the "stark horror" of the story with the "spiritual anguish" promised in the novel's epigraph from the Book of Job—"Even today is my complaint rebellious; my stroke is heavier than my groaning"—but he finally sees this anguish in terms of Wright rather than Bigger:

> This note of anguish, which emphasizes Bigger's suffering, is so intense as to be almost physical in character. It is sustained by a style which can only be called visceral. The author writes from his guts, describing the emotional state of his characters in graphic psychosomatic terms. It is a characteristic device which has its source in Wright's aching memory of the deep south.

The observation, as this essay attempts to demonstrate, is essentially true. But it is no less true that the critic here—and later in his essay as well—refuses to deal with the nature of Bigger's individuality as it comes to grips with itself. He winds up summing the novel's themes thus: "Bigger is a human being whose environment has made him incapable of relating meaningfully to other human beings except through murder." Surely this does not give much room to that "movement of the spirit" which Wright's epigraph from Scripture suggests that we seek. [Critic] Donald Gibson has addressed himself to this curious obtuseness of critics who fail to deal with the totality of the character, charging them with sociocultural blindness: "most critics of Wright's novel see only the outer covering of Bigger Thomas, the blackness of his skin and his resulting social role. Few have seen him as a discrete entity, a particular person, who struggles with the burden of his humanity."

Considered as more than a representative figure or pawn in a sociological murder-melodrama, Bigger's story extends from the brilliantly epitomic opening domestic scene to his dismissal of Max on the last page of the narrative, and not, as many of Gibson's "blind" readers would have it, from Mary Dalton's murder to Boris Max's defense. Bigger's purpose, the action which this novel imitates, is the search for identity, an identity denied him by both his social milieu and his family situation. Bigger seeks a world in which he is not an alienated being, a world in which he can be "at home." Bigger's severe alienation from his human environments is matched by a sensual awareness (expressed in what Bone calls Wright's "visceral" prose style) which develops a nearly philosophical intensity. Thus, Wright manages to replicate, through the experience of Bigger, his own experience in coming to terms with his imagination as the "at home" identity that would save him from the familial and social threat that surrounded him. In Bigger's case it is not a mediated and formalized form of aggression that is the instrument of liberation, but rather the unmediated, literal, and violent murders of Mary Dalton and Bessie Mears. . . .

No Man's Land

In considering the total action of *Native Son*—the psychic motive out of which the events are generated—as Bigger's effort "to discover an identity," the killing of white Mary Dalton, half-accidental and unconscious as it is, is secondary to the purposeful and free act of killing black Bessie Mears.

Mary Dalton's death is Dreiserian [characteristic of the writer Theodore Dreiser], determined by Bigger's social conditioning and the terrible pressure of the moment. Mary's clumsy efforts at social egalitarianism and Marxist comaraderie with her father's new chauffeur make only for confusion in Bigger's mind. He recoils from their attempts at intimacy, for it sharpens his shame and hatred of his status.

> He felt he had no physical existence at all right then: he was something he hated, the badge of shame which he knew was attached to a black skin. It was a shadowy region, a No Man's Land, the ground that separated the white world from the black that he stood upon. He felt naked, transparent; he felt that this white man (Jan Erlone), having helped to put him down, having helped to deform him, held him up now to look at him and be amused. At that moment he felt toward Mary and Jan a dumb, cold, and inarticulate hate.

Bigger feels vividly his condition of being "cut dead" by his social environment; Jan's and Mary's efforts at being friendly only exacerbate and intensify Bigger's sense of shame, fear, and hatred. The unreal, dreamlike quality of the murder scene later, comes into the tone of the novel here, with Bigger's uncomfortable journey across the city in the car, squeezed between Jan and Mary, who are completely blind to his terror. After the killing, Bigger realizes the absurdity: "It all seemed foolish! He wanted to laugh. It was unreal. He had to lift a dead woman and he was afraid. He felt that he had been dreaming of something like this for a long time, and then, suddenly, it was true."

Blindness and Invisibility

Killing Mary is thus clearly, for Bigger, a release of long pent-up aggressive tendencies that are both sexual and social. The act opens Bigger to a flood of realizations that he had managed all his life to repress with a half-conscious resistance. His vision cleared by his irreversible act, Bigger comes to grasp the essential blindness of both black and familial authority and white social authority. Having already grasped blind Mrs. Dalton's similarity to his mother and responded to it in kind, Bigger now sees that his own mother moves like a blind person, "touching objects with her fingers as she passed them, using them for support."

Bigger is elated by this perception of the essential blindness of all those who would censor and punish him for the as yet undiscovered murder. "His being black and at the bottom of the world was something which he could take with a newborn strength. What his knife and gun had once meant to him, his knowledge of having secretly murdered Mary now meant." But this sense of power does not satisfy him. Bigger finds that he wants to tell the world what he has done:

> He wanted the keen thrill of startling them.... He wished that he could be an image in their minds; that his black face and the image of his smothering Mary and cutting off her head and burning her could hover before their eyes as a terrible picture of reality which they could see and feel and yet not destroy.

Bigger's sense of his act of murder as a creative expression, as an act which confers on him a meaningful identity in his own eyes, is incomplete, even though "the knowledge that he had killed a white girl they loved and regarded as their symbol of beauty made him feel the equal of them, like a man who had been somehow cheated, but had now evened the score." Something more is required. Full psychic liberation can come to Bigger only when the image of his self reflected back at him by others coincides with his own image of his self. Although the knowledge of having murdered Mary Dalton replaces in his mind the sense of security that carrying a knife and a gun had given him,

> He was not satisfied with the way things stood now; he was a man who had come in sight of a goal, then had won it, and in winning it had seen just within his grasp another goal, higher, greater. He had learned to shout and had shouted and no ear had heard him; he had just learned to walk and was walking but could not see the ground beneath his feet; and had long been yearning for weapons to hold in his hands and suddenly found that his hands held weapons that were invisible.

Bessie Becomes Mother

[Literary critic] Charles James has pointed out that Bigger's girl, Bessie, "is the ear he needs to sound out the meaning of Mary's death. Through her, Bigger can gain some insight into his family's judgement of his act, without actually telling them." For Bessie is an oasis of motherly comfort in Bigger's world. Wright presents her and their essentially physical relationship in pastoral terms infused with stock female symbols—the "fallow field" and "the warm night sea" and the cooling and cleansing "fountain" whose "warm waters" cleared Bigger's senses "to end the tiredness and to reforge in him a new sense of time and space." This passive, maternal, all-accepting and sensually refreshing aspect of his mistress contrasts strongly in Bigger's mind with "the other Bessie," the questioning and censoring aspect of her which arouses in Bigger a desire "to clench his fist and swing his arm and blot out, kill, sweep away" all her resistance to his will and ideas.

Bessie's failure to understand and endorse the meaning Bigger has found in killing Mary Dalton dooms her. When

Bigger tells her what he has done, she is terrified that she will be implicated. Her near-hysterical outburst of weak fatalism contains an explicit rejection of Bigger's very being—"I wish to God I never seen you. I wish one of us had died before we was born"—and makes Bigger realize that she can neither accompany him on his flight, nor be left behind to betray him. Bessie has proven herself to be like his mother: weak, limited, blind. "He hated his mother for that way of hers that was like Bessie's. What his mother had was Bessie's whiskey, and Bessie's whiskey was his mother's religion." Bigger begins to conceive of killing Bessie as a free act, "as a man seeing what he must do to save himself and feeling resolved to do it."

Finding Self

Killing Bessie, Bigger comes closer than in killing Mary to direct expression of Richard Wright's own primary inner conflict, the desire to strike out against the women who limited, repressed, censored, and punished his rebellious initiatives. Having killed Bessie with a brick, Bigger feels at last "truly and deeply" free and alive. The killings have given him a sense of freedom, and he is now able to make a direct contact with that consciousness he had for so long held at arm's length: "he had killed twice, but in a true sense it was not the first time he had ever killed. He had killed many times before, but only during the last two days had this impulse assumed the form of actual killing." His elation now is larger than the pride and sense of power he derived from killing Mary. This time, with this murder, he is brought to the brink of a philosophical consideration of his identity. As Charles James provocatively puts it, having "symbolically 'wiped out' the progenitive elements of the two things he hates most [the white societal oppressor and the black, submissive oppressed]," Bigger is free to begin thinking as an existentially liberated person:

> But what was he after? What did he want? What did he love and what did he hate? He did not know. There was some-

thing he *knew* and something he *felt*; something the *world* gave him and something he *himself* had; something spread out in *front* of him and something spread out in *back*; and never in all his life, with this black skin of his, had the two worlds, thought and feeling, will and mind, aspiration and satisfaction, been together; never had he felt a sense of wholeness.

Killing Bessie Mears puts Bigger in the position of a questor, consciously searching for an identity—"a sense of wholeness"—that will enable him to "be at home" in his society, "to be a part of the world, to lose himself in it so he could find himself, to be allowed a chance to live like others, even though he was black." From this point forward no other action has greater meaning. After the newspaper headlines announce "*AUTHORITIES HINT SEX CRIMES*," Bigger feels alienation settle down around him again: "Those words excluded him utterly from the world." He knows now that the meaning of his acts will be denied by the whites in their blind fury to capture and kill him. The accusation of sexual violation denies the individuality of his action, "cuts him dead" again. He knows that white society will refuse to see and confirm his new sense of identity, his real self, which he created by murdering Mary and Bessie, the dual images of his psychosocial oppression. Murdering Bessie, Charles James argues, "is Bigger's acknowledgement of his own impending death. He knows he must be caught, so from that moment his energy is devoted to salvaging 'spiritual victory.'"

The ambiguity of Mary Dalton's death required, for Wright's satisfaction, an unambiguous and legitimate murder, for which Bigger can confess and be punished. Lest he again create a story that bankers' daughters might tearfully enjoy, he wedded the American, Dreiserian naturalist tradition and the Russian, Dostoevskian [characteristic of the Russian writer Fyodor Dostoevski] existential tradition to make Bigger's passion for murder as broadly meaningful as possible. . . .

Bigger's Spiritual Victory

When Bigger's crime career ends, and he is captured and brought bumpily down to earth, dragged by his ankles into the cold, white, enshrouding snow, he is forced to set aside the sense of power that the murders had given him. The motive which has impelled his behavior throughout, however—his drive to find a viable sense of identity—is not cast aside. It is in fact now his only concern. In the face of his impending death he must come to terms with his life, find some way to accept it, if he is to be "at home" in the world before he leaves it forever. The release of his repressive tension in the acts of murder was not useless; as in a dream, Bigger's expression of his internalized, repressed aggression makes subconscious data available to his conscious mind. As Bigger considers his end, then, the complex social considerations of Max's argument do not figure in his thought. Max's elaborate analogies and metaphors are lost on Bigger. The materials of Bigger's final meditations are his own perceptions of the world around him, freed from stereotype and threat by his murderous acts. The structure of book 3 is provided by Bigger's efforts to realize out of these materials a vision of social relatedness, a sense of his being and belonging in the world. He asks:

> If he reached out his hands, and if his hands were electric wires, and if his heart were a battery giving life and fire to those hands, and if he reached out with his hands and touched other people, if he did that, would there be a reply, a shock?

And in seeking an answer Bigger rejects the alternatives his life had presented to him. As Robert Bone notes, "He rejects his family ('Go home, Ma.'); his fellow prisoners ('Are you the guy who pulled the Dalton job?'); the race leaders ('They almost like white folks when it comes to guys like me.') and religion." His spiritual victory, if he is to have one, must come from within, be composed entirely of the stuff of the self. "He was balanced on a hairline now, but there was no one to push him forward or backward, no one to make him feel that he had any value or worth—no one but himself."

A Sense of Wholeness

Bigger comes through to a sense of identification with a human community at the very conclusion of his life and story. In his last conversation with Max, Bigger is calm and composed. . . . Max tries to give Bigger hope in a future collective human salvation, a Marxist vision of men reclaiming the world from their bosses. Bigger takes from what Max says confirmation of his new inner feeling, newly arrived at, that "at bottom all men lived as he had lived and felt as he had felt." Max tells him "the job in getting people to fight and have faith is in making them believe in what life has made them feel, making them feel that their feelings are as good as those of others." The feelings that Bigger accepts in himself are not, as so many critics have asserted, those of fear, shame, and hatred. But, as [American Marxist and scholar] Paul Siegel has recently noted, "it is hard to make men hear who will not listen. Seven times in the last page and a half of the novel Bigger cries out to Max, 'I'm all right,' the last time adding, 'For real, I am.'" Bigger is all right because, as he tries to tell Max, when he thinks about what Max has said he feels that he was right for wanting what he wanted—a sense of human integration, wholeness, identity.

> "They wouldn't let me live and I killed. Maybe it ain't fair to kill, and I reckon I really didn't want to kill. But when I think of why all the killing was, I begin to feel what I wanted, what I am. . . . I didn't want to kill . . . But what I killed for, I *am!* It must've been pretty deep in me to make me kill! . . . What I killed for must've been good. . . . I didn't know I was really alive in this world until I felt things hard enough to kill for 'em."

Now Siegel is too busy defending Max to take note of the fact that Bigger is not defending his hate and shame but rather the motive that lay behind all the actions of his short life—the unsatisfied drive to reject the negative identity that the cultural stereotypes had forced on him and to discover an adequate, integral replacement. Max, for all his good will, has never really seen Bigger's individual humanity. As Donald Gibson notes, he "cannot accept the implications of Bigger's conclusions, nor indeed, can he fully understand the position that Bigger has finally arrived at." As he departs Max gropes for his hat, "like a blind man." At the last Bigger speaks as a free man and equal human being not to Max, who can not, finally, look him in the eye, but to Jan. Jan has paid his dues, suffered, and learned to see Bigger as a human being.

The Black Male's Search for Identity in a Racist Society

Aimé J. Ellis

*Aimé J. Ellis is an assistant professor of African American litera-
ture at Michigan State University and the author of the 2009
book* If We Must Die: From Bigger Thomas to Biggie Smalls.

*Bigger Thomas represents the poor urban black male of the
1930s who suffered terrible abuses by society. From this perspective, Bigger's murderous rage can be understood, according to
Aimé J. Ellis. Ellis contends that for Bigger, the only place to vent
his pain and share his dreams was in the community of other
black males who shared his plight. But such socializing was often
played out through internalizing the ideals of the oppressor; that
is, white society, which then led to defiance and rebellion and,
ultimately, violence.*

Describing poor urban black life during the Great Depression of the 1930s, Wright's *Native Son* (1940) depicts
Chicago as a site of extreme racial and political violence.
Coupled with severe economic malaise as a result of the stock
market crash of 1929, conditions in the world of Wright's protagonist, Bigger Thomas, were largely indicative of white
America's racist and socially Darwinist disregard for black humanity. Indeed, as the literary historian Stephen Michael Best
has argued, "One could read causally the relation between de-
clining economic conditions and white terroristic violence,
suggesting that the former increased idleness and irritability
and led ultimately to the latter". For many young urban blacks
in northern ghettos of the 1930s, Bigger's violent rage was an
understandable, if not identifiable response to American racism and poverty.

Aimé J. Ellis, "'Boys in the Hood': Black Male Community in Richard Wright's
Native Son," *Callaloo* vol. 29, Winter, 2006, pp. 182–202. Copyright © 2006 The
Johns Hopkins University Press. Reproduced by permission.

Yet many cultural critics and writers would later dispute Bigger's representational value as an accurate depiction of the collective psyche of poor urban blacks during the 1930s. Indeed, in his well-known critique of Bigger Thomas in *Notes of a Native Son* (1955), the writer James Baldwin argues that "a necessary dimension has been cut away; this dimension being the relationship that Negroes bear to one another, that depth of involvement and unspoken recognition of shared experience which creates a way of life". To a large degree, Baldwin was right. Wright did not specifically elaborate on Bigger's relationships with other blacks or focus on the "ways in which Negroes are controlled in our society and the complex techniques they have evolved for their survival". Nevertheless, whether or not Wright explicitly acknowledged the importance of Bigger's relationships with other blacks, it is my contention that Bigger was immersed within a defiantly oppositional black male subculture that not only sought to insure his survival but also struggled to preserve his humanity.

Black Male Community

For Bigger and his friends (Gus, G.H., and Jack), Chicago's Black Belt afforded virtually no opportunities to gain access to industrial jobs or vocational training programs. Desperate to fight off hunger and feelings of despair, their daily routines consisted of raiding newsstands, fruit stands, and apartments, going to movies, hanging out at the local poolroom, or simply, "loafing around". A product of reform schools and the macho environment of the neighborhood poolroom, Bigger reflected the worst of "black male rage" and affirmed for many the prevalent stereotype of poor urban black males as irresponsible, savagely immoral, and inhumane. Even as Wright tells the story, Bigger was a bitter embodiment of the hatred of and injury inflicted on black people living in America's ghettos.

However unsavory Bigger's male world might have appeared, the social embraces and physical interactions that shaped the personality of his gang tell an important story concerning poor urban black male life. Surprisingly, few critics have sought to critically delve beyond what has been commonly perceived as a hypermasculine world of social despair and dysfunctional violence. Most often obscured in the critical scholarship of *Native Son*, Bigger's deeply emotional conversations with his homeboys constitute a site of black male community that allows them to purge the psychic pain of urban blight as well as symbolize an intimate space for sharing their dreams, aspirations, and joys. In an early scene of *Native Son*, Wright depicts a private moment between Bigger and Gus:

> Bigger took out his pack and gave Gus a cigarette; he lit his and held the match for Gus. They leaned their backs against the red brick wall of a building, smoking, their cigarettes slanting white across their black chins. To the east Bigger saw the sun burning a dappling yellow. In the sky above him a few white clouds drifted. He puffed silently, relaxed, his mind pleasantly vacant of purpose. Every slight movement in the street evoked a casual curiosity in him. Automatically, his eyes followed each car as it whirred over the smooth black asphalt. A woman came by and he watched the gentle sway of her body until she disappeared into a doorway. He sighed, scratched his chin and mumbled, "Kinda warm today.". . .

Playing White

Capturing what is rarely seen from outside the world of poor urban black males, Wright exposes in this scene an array of sentiments and emotions—playfulness, joy and pleasure, rage and frustration, fear and admiration, shame—that mark the complex intimacies and defiantly oppositional practices of black male homosociality [friendship between people of the same sex]. Bigger's persistent efforts to get Gus to "play white," for example, present us with a comical though disturbing moment in the text, a moment that both appropriates and subverts the oppressive social and political norms of the dominant culture. Indicative of a society in which black men are [according to scholar Abdul R. JanMohamed] "prevent[ed] from realizing their full potential as human beings and exclude[d] from full and equal participation in civil and political society," playing white is symptomatic of an attempted racial negation. Reenacting for themselves a world of power and control, Bigger and Gus resort to role-playing as white military leaders, as business executives, and as the president of the United States conferring with a high-level cabinet member. Gus, humoring Bigger, plays the part of the successful Wall Street investor:

> "This is J.P. Morgan speaking," Gus said. "Yessuh, Mr. Morgan," Bigger said; his eyes filled with mock adulation and respect. "I want you to sell twenty thousand shares of U.S. Steel in the market this morning," Gus said. "At what price, suh?" Bigger asked. "Aw, just dump 'em at any price," Gus said with casual irritation. "We holding too much." . . . "I bet that's just the way they talk," Gus said. "I wouldn't be surprised," Bigger said.

A few passages later, Bigger—acting as the president of the United States playfully addresses Gus as secretary of State:

> "Well, you see, the niggers is raising sand all over the country," Bigger said, struggling to keep back his laughter. "We've got to do something with these black folks. . . ." "Oh, if it's about the niggers, I'll be right there, Mr. President," Gus said.

Grasping White Patriarchy

What do these comedic displays of white authority and legitimacy mean for two downtrodden black males in Chicago's Black Belt of the 1930s? What do they suggest about the ways in which political domination, economic disenfranchisement, and racial negation effectively shape the psyches of poor urban black males? What do they say about that faraway and unwelcoming place Wright refers to in *Native Son* as a "cold and distant world; a world of white secrets carefully guarded"? Consider [psychiatrist and philosopher] Frantz Fanon's landmark study of the psychological effects of colonization on the oppressed:

> The settler's world is a hostile world, which spurns the native, but at the same time it is a world of which he is envious. We have seen that the native never ceases to dream of putting himself in the place of the settler—not of becoming the settler but of substituting himself for the settler. This hostile world, ponderous and aggressive because it fends off the colonized masses with all the harshness it is capable of, represents not merely a hell from which the swiftest flight possible is desirable, but also a paradise close at hand which is guarded by terrible watchdogs.

Inserting Bigger into Fanon's formulation as "the native [who] never ceases to dream of putting himself in the place of the settler" supplies us with a psychosocial lens for understanding how Bigger and Gus are subjects bound to repeat and mime the legitimating norms by which they have been degraded. Indeed, "play[ing] white" reflects a symbolic appropriation and "internalization" of the central attributes not simply of whiteness but of "white patriarchal power"—authority, property ownership, conquest, control—whereby Wright's native sons attempt to personify powerful white men as a means of escaping their own racial invisibility and impotence.

It is in this sense that "playing white" suggests a logic for grasping the overarching impact of white patriarchy that informs Bigger's own desperate attempt to gain agency. The cultural critic Kobena Mercer identifies this adoption of values as a process "which occurs when black men subjectively internalize and incorporate aspects of the dominant definitions of masculinity in order to contest the conditions of dependency and powerlessness which racism and racial oppression enforce". Indeed, the link between white patriarchal authority and violence within Bigger's black world cannot go understated. In both a psychic and imaginative sense Bigger and Gus lose themselves in a dangerous play of white manhood that will later play out in their violently aggressive social practices in the black community.

Defiance and Insurrection

At the same time, however, it seems necessary to appreciate how their performative skits of white male legitimacy and authority—full of sarcasm and insincerity—unfaithfully reenact those same legitimating norms. In effect their scrutinizing rendition of white male authority ("his eyes filled with mock adulation and respect") functions as a form of mimicry in which Bigger and Gus question, oppose, and ultimately attempt to subvert racial negation, subordination, and second-class citizenship. As [Professor] Farah Griffin's reading of Bigger attests, "The closest he [Bigger] gets to holding the power of the white man is through this game, and yet inherent in the game is a critique of white people". More often than not, however, these "games" reflect for Bigger and Gus both a sense of futility and racial impotence.

Nevertheless, it is from within this private and guarded space of black male homosociality that they struggle to create a sense of agency, self-worth, and meaning, a space from which they as black men attempt to carve out their own humanity. Unsatisfied by the relief that parodying white people affords, Bigger quickly becomes angry and yells out in frustration:

> "But I just can't get used to it," Bigger said. "I swear to God, I can't. I know I oughtn't think about it, but I can't help it. Every time I think about it I feel like somebody's poking a red-hot iron down my throat. Goddammit, look! We live here and they live there. We black and they white. They got

things and we ain't. They do things and we can't. It's just like living in jail. Half the time I feel like I'm on the outside of the world peeping in through a knothole in the fence."

Wright seems to have implicitly understood how Bigger's frustration in the above passage led to a practice of repudiation in which his inability or unwillingness to "get used to it [racial and class oppression]" illustrates the more prevalent way in which Bigger comes to assert his humanity. Thus the practice of "playing white" as a means for social critique and self-assertion is but one of several tactics employed by Bigger and his friends to combat racial terror and resist the trauma of negation and submission. Indeed other tactics or "life practices" that constitute sites of urban black male community are found in the subsequent pages of "Fear."

Take, for example, the plotting of the Blum robbery [and] the poolroom brawl between Gus and Bigger. In these defiantly oppositional practices, Bigger rejects second-class citizenship and partial assimilation into white America, finding empowerment and virtue through the embodiment of the racist sign and signifier, "nigger." In what cultural critic Abdul R. JanMohamed has called "negating the racist negation," Wright's poor urban black males—forced to conform to the negative stereotypes of a racist imagination—wear the mask of the nigger in a paradoxical move to defy the denigrating and self-effacing social and political norms prescribed to blacks during Jim Crow. That is to say, as Wright asserts in his own autobiography, "In what other way had the South allowed me to be natural, to be real, to be myself, except in rejection, rebellion, and aggression?" Thus whereas "masquerading" as niggers clearly reaffirms the mythologizing dominant discourse of white society, it can also be understood as a kind of performance of black male identity that reflects not only a sense of defeat and degradation but also (and most importantly here) a sense of defiance and insurrection.

Wright's Solution to Racism

Cynthia Tolentino

Cynthia Tolentino is an assistant professor of English at the University of Oregon and the author of the 2009 book America's Experts: Race and the Fictions of Sociology.

As Richard Wright pointed out after writing Native Son, *black Americans did not have a chance of full membership in their country unless the national culture was transformed. Instead of through race or money, Cynthia Tolentino notes, Wright proposed that blacks attain solidarity and power through labor. Tolentino points out that Wright also made a connection between American racism, German fascism, and old Russia's class struggle, claiming that while Bigger was an American product, he could have also been a creation of either communism or fascism. Within this context Wright formulates his vision, as opposed to social science models, of how to overcome racism in America.*

In *Native Son*, Wright explore[s] the possibilities for black subjectivity through the story of Bigger Thomas, a young black man whose first day as a chauffeur for the Daltons, a wealthy white family, culminates in the accidental murder of his employer's daughter. Through Bigger's encounters with members of the Dalton household, Wright considers the way in which the black subject is constructed by the disciplines of anthropology and sociology. If the novel offers a critique of liberal solutions to racism, however, it seems even more preoccupied with attempts by blacks to grapple with the constricted forms of subjectivity available to them in Jim Crow society. In examining the forms of individual agency consti-

Cynthia Tolentino, "The Road Out of the Black Belt: Sociology's Fictions and Black Subjectivity in *Native Son*," *Novel*, vol. 33, Summer 2000, pp. 377–406. Copyright © 2000 NOVEL Corp. Reproduced with permission.

tuted by black Americans through their engagement with liberal narratives of race, the novel outlines a new model for black subjectivity.

In a powerful scene that evokes wartime images of American political power and industrial development, Bigger and Gus watch a commercial plane circle the sky, leaving the advertisement "Use Speed Gasoline" in its trail. The dialogue that accompanies this image of two young black men passively watching the plane emphasizes their exclusion from a heroic narrative of modernity and progress. When Bigger insists to Gus, "I could fly a plane if I had a chance," Gus retorts, "If you wasn't black and if you had some money and if they'd let you go to that aviation school, you could fly a plane". In his remark, Gus lists race, class, and access to education as the set of exclusions that define for blacks the consequences of living in a racist and segregated culture. Not surprisingly, then, this scene silences the dramatic sweep of the message-bearing plane with the material reality of racism and poverty. While whites are viewed as the normative protagonists in modern American culture, blacks are figured as passive consumers and bystanders. This scene functions as an allegory of racial inequality that assumes that to be a modern American citizen one has to "become" a white American.

By giving voice to the racial privilege that undergirds narratives of modernity, this scene challenges the egalitarianism traditionally associated with representations of national progress. It also demonstrates the absence of self-possession, agency, and racial consciousness in Bigger and Gus, suggesting that they do not yet have the tools to analyze the circumstances of their disenfranchisement [i.e., being deprived of the rights of citizenship]! In particular, Bigger is described as having "in his eyes a pensive, brooding amusement, as of a man who had been long confronted and tantalized by a riddle whose answer seemed always just on the verge of escaping him, but prodding him irresistibly on to seek its solution". The scene stages—and short circuits—a discussion of racial subjugation in order to show how interpretations of racism remain incomplete. Indeed, Bigger's inability to fully comprehend the workings of racism implicit in Gus's response is asserted as a gap in knowledge that requires a "solution."

Exclusion from National Participation

While Wright exposes the falsity of America's egalitarian rhetoric by pointing out the exclusion of blacks from narratives of national progress, he also explores the terms that constitute nationalist affiliation and subjectivity. Having tired of watching the plane, Bigger persuades his friend Gus to play "White," a game in which they imitate the actions and manners of powerful white men. Taking on the roles of an Army general, financial tycoon J.P. Morgan, and the President of the United States, they act out scenes of authority borrowed from movies and other media associated with white men. In their performances, Bigger and Gus figure whiteness as heightened masculine authority and economic empowerment through which they are able to participate in public decision making, direct the allocation of financial resources, and discipline others.

Their performances of whiteness temporarily claim authority and agency in a way that reveals the fabricated nature of American subjectivity. By appropriating the words, gestures, and forms of entitlement that constitute white male authority, Bigger and Gus challenge the naturalized appearance of the white male subject. As [English academic] Richard Dyer reminds us, power "works in a particularly seductive way with whiteness, because of the way it seems rooted, in commonsense thought, in things other than ethnic difference". What Bigger and Gus expose in their game is the way in which black subjectivity is traditionally defined in a negative relation to white power and agency, thus throwing into question the possibility of black autonomy and agency within such a binary definition of racial difference.

While *Native Son* portrays the exclusion of African Americans from narratives of national progress [Wright's essay], "How Bigger Was Born" articulates a more specific role for them in the production of national culture. First, Wright considers how the criteria for membership and participation in the nation has been structured around race, claiming that African Americans "would dream of what it would be like to live in a country where they could forget their color and play a responsible role in the vital processes of the nation's life". In arguing that the inability of blacks to identify more closely with the national polity has contributed to their marginalization, he suggests that racial reform can be achieved through the creation of a new role for blacks in relation to national culture. Such a revision of the relationship of blacks to national culture hinges upon a new figuration of national culture, one in which blacks can identify as protagonists. What Wright proposes, then, is a form of nationalist affiliation that is based first upon labor solidarity rather than race. The dialectic that he outlines asserts that black identification with the class struggle will create the conditions through which racial consciousness, in the form of black unity and agency, will emerge.

Longing for Full Membership

If Bigger's job with the Daltons places him on the path to self-making and upward mobility, then his metamorphosis into a productive citizen is violently derailed by the murders of Mary and Bessie. The question that remains, however, is what alternative narrative takes shape where the developmental trajectory of the narrative of self-making leaves off. Through the narration of the events that lead up to Mary's death, the novel suggests that the crime is largely motivated by Bigger's confusion and fear over how he will be perceived as a black man. When he helps the intoxicated Mary to her room, he wonders "what a white man would think seeing him here with her like this?". The contradictory impulses that Mary's presence evokes for Bigger articulate the threat that white women carried for black men:

> He watched her with a mingled feeling of helplessness, admiration, and hate. If her father saw him here with her now, his job would be over. But she was beautiful, slender, with an air that made him feel that she did not hate him with the hate of other white people. But, for all of that, she was white and he hated her.

This description reveals the degree to which the symbolic presence of white women defined social boundaries for black men. Although a white woman is predominantly figured as an irreducible marker of race and a potential threat to the economic and physical survival of black men, it is important to note the way in which Bigger acknowledges differences between Mary and "other white people." This implies the possibility of interracial bonds as well as Bigger's inability to see racial difference as productive of social alliances rather than divisions.

Unlike the paths articulated by dominant liberal discourse for the incorporation of African Americans into the national polity, Wright argues that blacks can only imagine themselves as part of the nation through solidarity with other workers. For black Americans, he writes, there was "a wild and intense longing (wild and intense because it was suppressed!) to belong, to be identified, to feel that they were alive as other people were, to be caught up forgetfully and exultantly in the swing of events, to feel the clean, deep, organic satisfaction of doing a job in common with others". This "longing" for full membership in the nation is, according to Wright, synonymous with the desire for a shared feeling of productivity and progress with other workers. The alternative trajectory envisioned in this passage for the formation of black American subjectivity stakes out a new configuration of national culture that does not solely depend upon the assimilation of blacks into mainstream American society, but that requires a more extensive reorganization of American identity in terms of race and class. Indeed, for Wright, previous forms of black agency tended to serve the white and black bourgeoisie; he denounces, for example, the educated black middle classes who used their privilege to align themselves with the white bourgeoisie rather than to help poor blacks. Black Americans will only be able to take an active role in national culture through identification with a larger labor- and class-based network and political context.

Comparing Racism to Fascism

In his account of the genesis of Bigger Thomas, Wright tells us that his protagonist emerged from a recognition of similarities between racism in the United States and the rhetoric of fascism in Europe: "I was startled to detect, either from the side of the Fascists or from the side of the oppressed, reactions, moods, phrases, attitudes that reminded me strongly of Bigger, that helped to bring out more clearly the shadowy outlines of the negative that lay in the back of my mind". In a comparison of fascism in Germany to racism in the United States, he points to the Nazi preoccupation with the "construction of a society in which there would exist among all people (German people, of course!) one solidarity of ideals, one continuous circulation of fundamental beliefs, notions, and assumptions". Wright focuses here on the contradictions within a key element of classical liberalism, the notion of a civil society, or an alternative to a hierarchical social order, which both German fascism and American racism hold in common. At another moment, he compares the Nazi reliance upon rituals and symbols to the quest for black leaders in Marcus Garvey's "Back to Africa" movement. Although he rejects Garvey's separatist political agenda, he acknowledges the desire for a place in which blacks could be political leaders and participate in the nation as full citizens that inspired

Garvey's vision of remaking a "home" for black Americans in Africa. Wright calls attention to the cultural alienation that has produced a sense of estrangement in Bigger and notes that "the civilization that had given birth to Bigger contained no spiritual sustenance, had created no culture which could hold and claim his allegiance and faith".

By rewriting the traditional narrative in which America's uniqueness is defined through its opposition to Nazi fascism and Russian totalitarianism, Wright reveals the degree to which articulations of United States global power depend upon the separation of racism from international politics. The parallels that he sees in "the emotional tensions of Bigger in America and Bigger in Nazi Germany and Bigger in old Russia" challenge the dominant narrative of American exceptionalism. By appropriating the terms of opposition through which America's cultural and political coherence is achieved, Wright then uses them to argue that American democratic culture can be redeemed—and differentiated from Nazi Germany—through Bigger. Wright's belief that Bigger, "an American product, a native son of this land, carried with him the potentialities of either Communism or Fascism" places Bigger within an international context, implying that Bigger's political allegiance has not yet been articulated. Wright points out that the withholding of education and the effects of racism have prevented the formation of a collective political consciousness and solidarity amongst black Americans, leaving them in a "state of individual anger and hatred". As a "dispossessed and disinherited man," a product of a "dislocated society," Bigger must choose: whether he will "follow some gaudy, hysterical leader who'll promise rashly to fill the void in him, or whether he'll come to an understanding with the millions of his kindred fellow workers under trade-union or revolutionary guidance depends upon the future drift of events in America". In placing Bigger's destiny both in his own hands and those of the nation, Wright argues that whatever becomes of Bigger will not be in support of the liberal segregationist status quo. In focusing on the lack of education as a contributing factor to black inequality and the durability of racism, he implicitly suggests that collective black identity can be achieved through the consciousness-raising "guidance" of black intellectuals.

By emphasizing the similarities between German fascism, the class struggle in Russia, and American racism, Wright transforms these contexts into sources of political strength for black Americans. As he explains, the political unrest that resulted in the development of German fascism can be compared to the discontent of black Americans with American society. Similarly, the "Russian principle of self-determination" makes visible the "longing for self-identification" of black Americans. By placing black Americans in continuity with Germany and Russia, Wright challenges the myth of American egalitarianism.

Black Political Consciousness

Charged with the historical mission of linking Bigger to international political movements, Wright asks, "Who will be the first to touch off these Bigger Thomases in America, white and black?". He then describes *Native Son* as an examination of the future of African Americans that has as much authority, if not more, than studies being carried out by white American social scientists:

> [W]hy should I not try to work out on paper the problem of what will happen to Bigger? Why should I not, like a scientist in a laboratory, use my imagination and invent test-tube situations, place Bigger in them, and following the guidance of my own hopes and fears, what I had learned and remembered, work out in fictional form an emotional statement and resolution of this problem?

By juxtaposing his literary exploration of Bigger in *Native Son* with scientific studies of the "Negro problem," Wright asserts his authority to offer an account of racism and its solution. Closely mirroring sociological challenges to biological and essentialist views of race, his interpretive authority draws from both scholarly knowledge and his "lived experience" as a black man in the United States. What separates *Native Son* most markedly from the sociological studies of race in the thirties is the way in which Wright posits blacks as the central protagonists of American social reform. While liberal narratives of race have traditionally figured black Americans as the subjects and beneficiaries of racial reforms carried out by white Americans, Wright's focus on the different forms of black agency constituted within the restrictions of Jim Crow society represents an important historical intervention in the ascription of social and developmental roles in liberal discourse. Instead of viewing the moral reform of white Americans as the primary weapon in the fight against racial bigotry, Wright turns attention to the development of political consciousness and agency in black Americans.

No Solidarity with the Oppressed

Damon Marcel DeCoste

Damon Marcel DeCoste is an associate professor of English at Regina University in Canada.

Even as Bigger Thomas resented whites and their oppression of him as a black man, he found himself identifying with the white world. Bigger longed for the world of glitter he witnessed through Hollywood films, magazines, newspapers, and radio. At the same time, Damon Marcel DeCoste argues, Bigger's shame of self translated into shame for others like him, including for his family and his buddies at the pool hall. Seeing them as poor and weak, Bigger did not want to be associated with them; nor did he want anything to do with Communists and other poor whites, because they had no money or power either.

Wright's Bigger Thomas is, as we first meet him, an unemployed black man of twenty, living in a one-room, rat-infested kitchenette with his mother, brother, and sister, and rankling at the restrictions placed upon his life by the tenets and practices of American racism. Indeed, at the outset of the novel, Bigger is presented as a very acute observer of the realities of American racism. As Bigger complains to Gus, his partner in petty crime, "They don't let us do nothing", but, apparently, make whites money. For as Bigger knows, the lines of race that cordon off the squalid South Side are ones that turn a profit for those white landlords and shopkeepers who live elsewhere. Bigger knows "that black people could not go outside of the Black Belt to rent a flat," and knows moreover

Damon Marcel DeCoste, "To Blot It All Out: The Politics of Realism in Richard Wright's *Native Son*," *Style*, vol. 32, Spring 1998, pp. 127–129. Copyright © 1998 Northern Illinois University. All rights reserved. Reproduced by permission of the publisher.

that, so caged, they pay twice the rent whites do for their slum dwellings. Indeed, as he muses sardonically to himself, even bread is one cent more expensive in South Side grocery stores.

Bigger's Reality

Everywhere Bigger's aspirations turn, these same lines loom, keeping him, in every sense, in his place, and he knows only too well the risks attendant upon straying from this place. As he walks through a wealthy white neighbourhood, Bigger understands fully that he is a target here, a figure perceived as a threat, a criminal, the dread black rapist of Southern lynch-mob rhetoric: "Suppose a police saw him wandering in a white neighborhood like this? It would be thought he was trying to rob or rape somebody". His boyhood dreams of being a pilot or a soldier have run into this same barrier, the school of aviation barring black students as the army of Uncle Sam admits them only "to dig ditches" and "scrub floors". Thus the lessons young Bigger has learned well are ones of his own imprisonment, of American blacks being yoked to the service of the white world. As he himself articulates his experience of African-American reality, white Americans "own the earth [and] say black folks are dogs. They don't let you do nothing but what they want".

Yet if Bigger knows these facts of his own oppression, his response is an attempt to erase this reality, to deny its status as fact and to retreat to a position where its factuality cannot reach him. Rankling at his own circumscribed existence, Bigger withdraws from it, from the world that rebukes him, from those other blacks as sorry and powerless as he, finally from his own consciousness of the real itself. Indeed, because of what he knows of this reality, Bigger pursues a studied rejection of it:

> He shut [his family's] voices out of his mind. He hated his family because he knew that they were suffering and that he was powerless to help them. He knew that the moment he

A *"colored only"* store in the South, circa 1925. MPI/Hulton Archive/Getty Images.

allowed himself to feel to its fullness how they lived, he would be swept outside of himself with fear and despair. So he held toward them an attitude of iron reserve; he lived with them, but behind a wall, a curtain. And toward himself he was even more exacting. He knew that the moment he allowed what his life meant to enter fully into his consciousness, he would either kill himself or someone else. So he denied himself and acted tough.

Denying Reality

What is most remarkable in this passage is the portrait of an existence that is its own self-conscious negation. Bigger, who knows only too well the limits placed on his existence, assiduously obliterates such knowledge from his mind, denying both the suffering of those closest to him and his own frustration. Thus if Bigger is proffered as a character of acute insight into the realities of American racism, he is one also in deliberate flight from these realities.

Indeed, Bigger only lives by a process of erasing his own life. Anxious always "to do something to evade looking so squarely at this problem", he strives towards a denial of it that is its ostensible eradication. Thus the desire, indeed the phrase, predominant in Bigger's tale is that of "blotting it out." Squirming awkwardly in the face of Mr. Dalton's questioning, Bigger aches "to wave his hand and blot out the white man who was making him feel this". Caught in the Daltons' car by the friendly overtures of Mary Dalton and her Communist boyfriend, Jan Erlone, he yearns "to seize some heavy object and grip it with all the strength of his body and in some strange way rise up and stand in naked space above the speeding car and with one final blow blot it out—with himself and them in it". Faced with the claustrophobic existence of his family, he longs not only for a curtain behind which to hide, but also "to wave his hand and blot them out", erasing them as he would those whites who befuddle and terrify him. Bigger's persistent desire is for the wholesale erasure of a reality he cannot bear to acknowledge, for the obliteration not only of the whites who oppress, but of those blacks with whom he suffers, of, indeed, his own existence itself.

Denial's Outlet

And this desire has, in Wright's novel, its readily available outlet. If Bigger yearns for something that will enable him to forget his own circumstances, this longing is met in *Native Son* by popular media catering precisely to the wish for fantasy rather than realism. As [scholar] Ross Pudaloff notes, Bigger's world is one "dominated by movies, magazines, newspapers and detective stories", and it is indeed toward these media that Bigger hungrily turns. What they offer him is precisely that for which he longs, an erasure of world that is also an erasure of self. Thus leaving his family's flat, restless and dissatisfied even with his imminent job interview at the Dalton home, Bigger aches "to see a movie; his senses hungered for it. In a movie he could dream without effort; all he had to do was lean back in a seat and keep his eyes open". The appeal here is twofold: movies are desired both because they offer dreams rather than that knowledge of reality which only torments him and because they are the kind of dreams requiring no dreamer, because they permit that erasure of self Bigger so desires. Such movies, and with them the pulp fiction of detective magazines, the sensational headlines of the Chicago dailies, and the lyrics of the latest dance tune, provide Bigger with a dream, a diversion, itself powerful enough to suppress the facts of his life. This indeed, as Bigger himself articulates it, is the very heart of their desirability: "He longed for a stimulus powerful enough to focus his attention and drain off his energies. He wanted to run. Or listen to some swing music. Or laugh or joke. Or read a *Real Detective Story* magazine. Or go to a movie".

But if Bigger longs for such stimuli as an erasure of self and world, what these media in fact present him with is an alternative world, a vision of an existence beyond his experience but not, thanks to these conventional sources, his ken. What Bigger finds, and indeed loves, in the movie-house and pulp magazine is a portrait of life defined not, as is his own, by limitations, poverty, and impotence, but rather by possibility, wealth, and power. Bigger's immersion in popular culture thus emerges here not only as a denial of the realities of his own oppression, his own experience, but also as an identification with and endorsement of the wealth and power of those who oppress him. Happily watching the matinee newsreels, Bigger sees a world of white American luxury, a world of "the daughters of the rich taking sun baths in the sands of Florida," a sight that, the commentator informs him, "represents over four billion dollars of America's wealth". Next to this vision, both his own experience and the feature film's portrait of "naked black men and women whirling in wild dances" recede into insignificance. Bigger's mind is instead occupied with an awe-filled longing for that other world, that "real" world of Hollywood fantasies. Consciousness of self and world, as indeed of the black "savages" of B-movies, is here "replaced by images in his own mind of white men and women dressed in black and white clothes, laughing, talking, drinking and dancing". Not only Trader Horn's African scene, but his own experience as a black American are effectively occluded by media-fostered dreams of a white world, a "realer" because desired reality of opulence and power.

Identifying with the Oppressor

But for Wright as realist, this erasure of self and world represents only Bigger's schooling in submission, an endorsement of the power others hold over him. In *Native Son* to accept the dream, to eschew realism, is only to perpetuate the realities of oppression. In Bigger's eyes, then, those well-dressed whites of his movie-house fantasies are "smart people; they knew how to get hold of money, millions of it". The wealth and power of white America become here, in Bigger's attempts to blot out his reality, his own standards of value. In his mass media evasion, Bigger ends up not only retreating from his world, his people, indeed himself, but identifying himself with those powerful whites who, as he knows, will not let him do anything. Scorning poor whites as "stupid" for their inability to get hold of millions Bigger spends his free time "playing white," assuming the roles of J.P. Morgan, the President, and white generals, speaking lines "heard . . . in the movies". Having found his proper objects of respect and value in the wealthy whites he himself knows to own the earth, Bigger seeks a final erasure of himself in the dream of being these whites, of dispensing with their wealth, of making their decisions, of, indeed, dealing in their fashion with "the niggers . . . raising sand all over the country". Thus if, as Wright himself describes him, Bigger is a man "trying to react to and answer the call of the dominant civilization whose glitter [comes] to him through newspapers, magazines, radios, movies", he is one also who makes his answer by assenting to the values of those who oppress him, by, indeed, contradicting and denying the reality he suffers.

For the Marxist Wright of 1940, this assent, of course, is no strange phenomenon. As he himself, paraphrasing [Marxist Russian leader Vladimir] Lenin, wrote in 1938, "oppressed minorities often reflect the techniques of the bourgeoisie more brilliantly than some sections of the bourgeoisie themselves. The psychological importance of this becomes meaningful when it is recalled that oppressed minorities ... strive to assimilate the virtues of the bourgeoisie in the assumption that by doing so they can lift themselves into a higher social sphere". While we shall soon see how Bigger himself, after his accidental killing of Mary Dalton, makes this assumption, what is most important in this identification is how it feeds both Bigger's own sense of terror and powerlessness in the face of white America and his alienation from all those—his fellow blacks, the poor whites, "Reds" like Jan and Boris Max—with whom he might struggle not to evade but to change the world. Certainly Bigger's identification with the wealth and power of the oppressor leads to a contempt for those whites who will not play this role. Of the Communists who will become first his scapegoats and then his defenders, Bigger has only the vaguest, most caricatured of notions, one gleaned from that mass media dream-world with which he blots out his experience: "He remembered seeing many cartoons of Communists in newspapers and always they had flaming torches in their hands and wore beards and were trying to commit murder or set things on fire. People who acted that way were crazy". Yet if Bigger has learned through newspaper stereotypes that the "Reds" are crazy, what most repels him is their manifest lack of identification with that world he himself holds dear. As Bigger sees it, the problem with the "Reds," as with the stupid poor whites, is precisely their exclusion from the world of wealth and power: "He didn't want to meet any Communists. They didn't have any money".

Shame of Self

If Bigger's scorn thus reveals a contempt for the common, for those who share in some sense that world of dispossession and disempowerment which is his own, this contempt is all the more acute and alienating in Bigger's relations with other African Americans. For at the heart of Bigger's admiration for the white world captured in matinee newsreels is, as we have seen, a hatred for, the desire to erase, his own poverty and powerlessness. Bigger retreats behind a curtain in his dealings with other blacks because, identifying with wealth and power, he can see in others like himself only contemptible weakness, indeed only a reflection of that position he occupies and loathes. Bigger's dealings with his family, "friends," and lover, then, are all governed by feelings of shame and self-hatred, feelings bound up in his education in, and identification with, the values of wealth and power learned in newspapers and movie houses. Toward the family for whom he announces his contempt at the very opening of the novel Bigger can feel only a scornful pity and shame. Even as they weep and plead for him as he awaits trial, Bigger can only recoil in disgust at what he sees as the revelation of that weakness he wants to erase. They are for him no solace, but rather only the badge of his shameful impotence, something therefore to be obliterated, denied: "Bigger wanted to whirl and blot them from sight. . . . He felt that all of the white people in the room were measuring every inch of his weakness. He identified himself with his family and felt their naked shame".

If Bigger here "identifies" with his family, it is only in terms of ascribing to them that shame and loathing he feels, a shame and a loathing that stem rather from his identification with the scorn he sees in the eyes of white onlookers. This dynamic of loathing and withdrawing from those who suffer as he does governs all of Bigger's relations with other African Americans, such that his dealings with them become rehearsals of rejection. Bigger does not "think enough of" the gang with whom he pulls his petty heists to care what they think of him, or ever to attempt to explain himself to them. Likewise, toward his "girl," Bessie, he feels, as he admits to Communist lawyer Boris Max, neither love nor hate; she is, in his own words, "just my girl. I don't reckon I was ever in love with nobody. . . . You have to have a girl, so I had Bessie". And, indeed, precisely insofar as this compulsory "girl" assumes a human significance, a black face and a black life like his own, she is to be denied: "he felt that there were two Bessies: one a body that he had just had and wanted badly again, the other was in Bessie's face; it asked questions. . . . He wished he could clench his fist and swing his arm and blot out, kill, sweep away the Bessie on Bessie's face and leave the other helpless and yielding before him". With family, friends and lover, Bigger can only re-enact that erasure of self he pursues throughout the novel, an eradication of a reality that is for him, looking on it through an admiration for and identification with a white American dream, not only unbearable but contemptible. What is to be sought instead is an identification with the oppressor in such dreams, an identification that may permit Bigger's assertion of difference from the weak and indeed from himself, but that marks the death of the very possibility of solidarity with the oppressed: "There were rare moments when a feeling and longing for solidarity with other black people would take hold of him. . . . [B]ut that dream would fade when he looked at the other black people near him. Even though black like him, he felt there was too much difference between him and them to allow for a common binding and a common life".

Bigger's Helpless Fear

Yet if Bigger's rejection of the reality he knows thus significantly sounds the death knell for any possibility of unity with those like himself, his admiration for the affluent whites of Hollywood film leads him to actual assaults on other blacks and, indeed, to that barely conscious act, the killing of Mary Dalton, which is his own undoing. For if Bigger is awestruck in the face of those wealthy white figures in his movie-house dreams, it is awe holding terror as well as admiration, a terror which leads him to an actual and violent blotting out of black victims—and ultimately of himself. The white world with which he seeks to erase his own experience figures in Bigger's imagination no longer as a social system or an aggregate of individuals, but as a powerful, indeed fearsome, natural force; it is for him both the paradise of power and wealth and "that looming mountain of white hate," something both inhuman and terrifying in that very power he covets in it. Moreover, although Bigger himself sees this fearsomeness as somehow different from his imagining of this world in the pre-fabricated dreams of American cinema, his schooling there in an identification with the powerful white force that hates itself is also an education in terror before this force. While Bigger, when confronted with Mary Dalton in the flesh rather than in her celluloid projections, muses "in amazement how different the girl had seemed in the movie. On the screen she was not dangerous and his mind could do with her as it pleased", the lesson he leaves the theatre having learned is one of fear rather than of empowerment. Identifying with the white power and affluence on the screen, Bigger becomes increasingly anxious about his gang's imminent robbery of a white man and leaves the theatre "with a mounting feeling of fear". The mythical world with which he attempts to blot out himself and those like him becomes, in this very attempt, "a sort of great natural force, like a stormy sky looming overhead, or like a deep swirling river stretching suddenly at one's feet". It is as such a mythic force that this world becomes the motive behind the violence Bigger enacts on those closest to himself.

For having learned the lesson not only of an admirable and validated white pre-eminence, but also of the fearsome character of this pre-eminence, Bigger's first concern is to derail that "violation of ultimate taboo"—his gang's plan to rob Blum's Deli. What this derailment significantly involves is violence against other blacks, those "friends" with whom he commits his petty crimes. As cohort Gus appears at the appointed time, making the robbery an imminent reality, Bigger, gripped by terror, not only assaults him, but pulls a knife on him and makes him, on his knees and helpless, lick it. This whole performance, the beating and humiliation of another African American, is both the result of Bigger's own helpless fear before the endorsed white power of his dreams and itself a blotting out or covering up of this fear, both for their and his own benefit: "His confused emotions made him feel instinctively that it would be better to fight Gus and spoil the plan of the robbery than to confront a white man with a gun. But he kept this knowledge of his fear thrust firmly down in him; his courage to live depended on how successfully his fear was hidden from his consciousness". Bigger's violence issues not only from his own persistent need to erase what he knows to be the case, but also from that denied fear which is itself the product of this attempt. Moreover, as with his early drawing of that curtain which separates him from his family, the result here is not only a bleeding and humbled Gus, but a Bigger Thomas once more cut off from those closest to, and most like, himself: "he knew that what had happened today put an end to his being with them in any more jobs".

Bigger's Sense of Superiority

Lale Demirtürk

Lale Demirtürk is an associate professor in the Department of American Culture and Literature at Bilkent University in Turkey.

According to Lale Demirtürk, Bigger, in killing Mary Dalton, felt a twofold power over the whites before whom he used to feel powerless. First, when he killed Mary, her ability to manipulate him was gone. Next, in knowing that whites did not believe a black man was capable of pulling off such a crime, Bigger felt empowered knowing he had done it. In contrast, Bigger's killing of Bessie represented his desire to kill his own image, his blackness. In the end, even as the white community recognized what he had done, they did not recognize his individuality, viewing him only as a "black ape."

[In] Wright's *Native Son*, Bigger's killing of Mary has given [him] a chance to reverse the power relationship between Mary and himself: for the first time he has been able to destroy the dominant image of the whites. No longer will Mary be able to manipulate his powerless image. By burning her corpse in the furnace to hide his crime, he can triumph over the white myth of black as totally powerless to act without white manipulation. Bigger finds power in white blindness to the individuality of a black person, in the whites' stereotypical images of blacks. That Bigger has done something that the whites do not know about provides him with a sense of superiority over them, regardless of the fact that the whites see him as inferior. He has now reversed the master-slave relationship between the Daltons and himself, for he has victimized the oppressor and has controlled the situation of which they are ignorant.

Lale Demirtürk, "Mastering the Master's Tongue: Bigger as Oppressor in Richard Wright's *Native Son*," *The Mississippi Quarterly*, vol. 50, Spring 1997, pp. 267–277. Copyright © 1997 Mississippi State University. Reproduced by permission.

His counter-stereotyping of whites is his defiance of white power in image-formation. In his intentional counter-blindness to Mary through the process of stereotyping, he has made himself into an image-destroyer. He has long wanted to blot out all the images of whites as objects of fear in his life in order to erase fear from both his mind and life: "To Bigger and his kind white people were not really people; they were a sort of great natural force". He has found considerable freedom in attacking the very image that functions as the mere justification of his exclusion from the white definitional framework. He has turned the image of Mary into the image of a victim who has lost control of the situation and therefore he "felt that he had his destiny in his grasp". He has also killed the referential meanings of Mary, Jan, Mr. and Mrs. Dalton that create shame, fear and hate in him. His sense of powerlessness in the face of the taboos against his social conduct/ status and sexuality that wipe the spirit of life out of his body is now replaced with the power he feels from violating those taboos, however covert the act of violation may be: "The knowledge that he had killed a white girl they loved and regarded as their symbol of beauty made him feel the equal of them, like a man who had been somehow cheated, but had now evened the score". He has been deprived of being any symbol of beauty, because his skin color has been the symbol of absence in the white society. He has now used his chance to kill the symbol that the white oppressor created in Mary: "Bigger Thomas," Houston A. Baker, Jr., points out, [in "Racial Wisdom and Richard Wright's *Native Son*"] "struck America's most sensitive nerve; he attacked the white female, its 'symbol of beauty.'" The white oppressor's image of beauty represents the very image of oppression for him. The whites' admiration for their object of purity and beauty has meant the rigid control of the black image of beauty and sexuality.

Control or Be Controlled

The private detective Britten's questions directed to Bigger about Mary and Jan reveal his stereotypical images of the blacks. Britten's remark "To me, a nigger's a nigger" reinforces Bigger's stereotyping of whites: "Britten was familiar to him; he had met a thousand Brittens in his life". His slander points to Jan as the potential murderer because he is a communist, and it reveals Bigger's ability to manipulate the stereotypical images of the white man. His wish to project his own fear of the white world onto whites like Jan and Britten reveals his repressed desire to shake the whites' image of him as submissive. He functions according to the white definitional framework as he writes the kidnap note. It is not only the murder or the kidnap note that "evens his score" with the whites, but also the clever manipulation—a white weapon long used against the blacks—through which he can match his wits with those of the whites. When the success of his manipulation of the stereotypical images of blacks is threatened by Bessie's fear, he has to kill her. Unlike Mary's accidental murder, Bessie's murder is an intentional one to prevent her telling on him. Since Bessie is in the same boat sharing the same lot with Bigger, he identifies himself with her, as opposed to Mary. He kills Bessie, for she represents his own self-image—his own blackness—to him. As Darwin T. Turner contends [in "The Outside: Revision of an Idea"]: "Bigger himself has escaped from the insecurities, the fears, the feelings of inferiority etched into the Negro psyche by centuries of repression in a white-dominated society. In Bessie, he sees a continuation of those mental chains. She is still lazily amoral, timid, compliant—in short, the Sambo personality which threatens the existence of the new Bigger. In order to live, Bigger must destroy her, the last link which reminds him of and binds him to his Negroness."

On the one hand he lets the whites—the Daltons, Peggy, Britten, the Press—feel that they control him because they control his image, but on the other he controls his own life by controlling his own image outside of their frame of reference. In either case the whites and Bigger are not equals, for while he can violate the imagery of domination, by not fitting into it, he cannot change the mental set of white labelling that determines the social space he is confined to. Bigger is surrounded by the people whose stereotypical images work against his manipulation of these images: Bigger is "just like all the other colored boys" to Peggy; "just another black ignorant Negro" to the reporters; the "Negro rapist and murderer" to the police; "black ape" to the white people who yell at him. The newspapers set the rhetoric of their image-domination: "Police . . . feel that the plan of the murder and kidnapping was too elaborate to be the work of a Negro mind". Against these various forms of stereotyping we have Bigger's pride in achieving freedom of action and opening up a personal space for himself: the murder of Mary produces "a possible order and meaning in his relations" with the whites, but the relationship creates meaning only for him, not for the whites, because they still refuse to see Bigger as an individual. Once his crime is clear and he is arrested by the police, Bigger's image is controlled by the Press. The *Tribunal*'s images of Bigger—"like an ape"/"a jungle beast"—remind us of the actual imagery of the *Chicago Tribune* clips of Robert Nixon [an eighteen-year-old black man convicted of rape and murder in 1938] from which Wright borrowed. The stereotypical images of blacks—such as "just like an ape," "giant ape," "animal," "jungle Negro," connoting the racist perception of the black as "beast/savage"; "rapist," as the sexual threat to white women; "criminal," as the primitive outlaw; and "moron" with no intellectual capacity—form a colonialist design for Bigger to fit into as the carbon-copy of all blacks.

Bigger Thomas:
Radical Revolutionary

Petar Ramadanovic

*Petar Ramadanovic is an associate professor of English at the
University of New Hampshire and author of* Forgetting Futures:
On Meaning, Trauma, and Identity.

*It is true that Bigger Thomas was a product of the racist society
in which he lived and that the racism Bigger dealt with was
twofold: racism of the mob and racism of the law. But Bigger
was more than a simple by-product of racism. According to Petar
Ramadanovic, Bigger was a radical agent, a revolutionary, in his
own right. For this, Bigger was willing to die. This explains why
he did not flee. In fleeing, Bigger would have given up his core
identity as revolutionary and as America's native son/native
alien.*

[W]right's Bigger] Thomas lives in a racist society, but
there are two qualitatively different racisms in [*Native Son*] and, therefore, there are two fundamentally different
ways to understand what and who a "black man" is in *Native
Son*. The first racism, which we could term post–Civil War
racism, is epitomized in the rule of the mob, and is a kind of
racism that is not considered legal in 1930's Chicago. This is
the racism Wright tries to escape in [his autobiography] *Black
Boy*; it is present in *Native Son* as a background to the kind of
racism that is formulated during the trial, in the last book of
the novel where Thomas's fate acquires its final form.

Racism and the Law

According to the prosecutor's winning argument, Bigger Thomas has jeopardized the very institution of the law—the law

Petar Ramadanovic, "*Native Son*'s Tragedy: Traversing the Death Drive with Bigger
Thomas," *Arizona Quarterly*, vol. 59, Summer 2003, pp. 81–106. Copyright © 2003
by the Regents of the University of Arizona. Reproduced by permission of the
publisher and the author.

that, in Buckley's words, "makes us human". Buckley uses Thomas's trial to draw a legal boundary between the human and the inhuman, "us" and "them," a divide that runs along racial lines. During the trial, we see, therefore, how mob rule comes to be replaced by the American judicial and penal systems.

After Thomas is sentenced, it is the institution of the law and the apparatus of power it can mobilize on its behalf—not the rule of the mob—that stands between white and black communities, protecting the former from a perceived, or fantasized, threat from, in Buckley's words, "some half-human black ape" who "may be climbing through the windows of our homes to rape, murder, and burn our daughters!" Buckley's argument does one more thing: it inverts the historical roles of perpetrator and victim. In his argument, whites suffer precisely those brutalities—rape, murder, and burning—that African American people suffered at the hands of whites during slavery and in its aftermath.

The inscription of mob rule and of the supremacist stereotype or fantasy in the law during Thomas's trial is the crucial reason why Buckley does not want to turn Thomas over to the white crowd asking for the black man's blood in front of the courthouse. Though the effect would be, in practical terms, the same, the legal ritual leading to Thomas's execution has a fundamentally different significance and consequence. The trial places the allegedly impartial courtroom at the very center of race relations. The trial thus represents the culminating phase—the phase in which we still live—in the long history of American racism, where the legal sphere becomes the primary site of the regulation and definition of race, as opposed to the social or economic spheres. The force behind the law is no longer the white mob, but the state's apparatus of power: its police, National Guard, military, its courts, prisons, etc.

Thus, that Thomas is a "black man" can be deduced only after Thomas is caught for the Dalton murder and brought to trial, for it is only then that his deed and the new definition of what black men are merge. Only after this event does Bigger Thomas become a "black man" in one of the two senses of the term argued during the trial, either Buckley's supremacist sense ("black men" are inhuman), which wins out, or Max's liberal sense ("black men" are products of a certain society), which will be legally represented years later in the Civil Rights Act of 1964 and the ensuing Affirmative Action programs designed, in the words of the United States Commission on Civil Rights, to "provide redress, however belated, for past practices of racial exclusion."

A Radical Agent

We can then say that Thomas's rebellion fails at the end of the novel because he is recognized not as the singular being called "Bigger Thomas," but only as a member of a group called "black men" in either Buckley's or Max's sense; and that, therefore, Wright's novel fails because it does not finally affirm its protagonist's struggle to affirm his being. Yet, to judge Thomas in these terms is to assign a specific nature to his act; namely, that his act could have been successfully accomplished in the U.S., and that Thomas had an opportunity to succeed in his self-realization. Since his act is neither an individual project, nor an ego-realization on the order of "be all that you can be"; since, more importantly, Thomas lets himself be caught, we are forced to look elsewhere for the full scope of his singular, tragic act, and for the significance of Thomas's death.

To reduce Thomas to predetermination by a racist society . . . or to understand his struggle as an individualistic act is to overlook the fact that Thomas is a revolutionary, radical agent and that this agency, this affirmation of life that transcends his ego, is so essential to him, to who he *is*, that he is willing to die for it.

Native Alien

Returning to the scene of his crime, Thomas deliberates about running away. He feels "caught up," consumed by a "supreme and meaningful act" and postpones making his decision whether to flee to a later moment. That moment, as we know from book two of *Native Son*, titled "Flight," never comes, and it seems that Thomas has not found a good reason to run away. We can then say that this native son is also "caught up" in the sense that he has no away toward which he can run, no other home but America.

As a tragic hero, Thomas has to show that he is aware that he has the option to flee and thus try to change his fate. But, at the same time, in order to be a tragic hero, he cannot exercise this possibility, and must proceed on his way toward his final doom. . . . Only by remaining on his path can Thomas affirm his being and, further, it is only if Thomas stays in America that the affirmation of his being can have an impact on America. If he runs away, he would cease to be Bigger Thomas, a native son and the country's illegitimate offspring, and he would give up the possibility of opening the system onto a logic, genealogy, and identity that are radically different from anything the system would or could acknowledge. Only if he stays can he make himself into what he already is, a *native alien* from whom the American system has tried to protect itself ever since, figuratively speaking, the first slave ships arrived on this continent.

What Thomas chooses to do when he postpones his flight can then be described in the following way: he attempts to strike at the system, to blot out its founding assumptions and myths, and, seeking recognition, to show that his being cannot be affirmed in his native land—not even by the most progressive ideology of the day. In order for Wright to show this, Thomas has to let the police catch him.

Once Thomas is caught, we could say that even Richard Wright pulls back from the monster he has created. After Max enters his cell, Wright makes this radical revolutionary—who thus far has rejected everyone around him—believe that he has been understood, and we see Thomas ready to submit to the authority of the benevolent, fatherly Jewish man. But Wright does not give in all the way; Thomas's appeal of the death penalty is refused, and he is left alone in the cell to meet his death, which is both the moment of Thomas's end and his triumph. After he is sentenced, he will die as a radical, and in this final act, in this act that defines all of his other acts, he will become what he is. The radical nature of Thomas's self-annihilating goal, this threatening "no" to both the white and black communities, is the crucial reason Wright occupies an ambiguous place in American and, more importantly, African American literature.

CHAPTER 3

Social Issues in Literature

Contemporary Perspectives on Civil Rights

Racism Continues in the South

Faye Fiore

Faye Fiore is a staff writer for the Los Angeles Times.

In the following article, Faye Fiore reports that while the overall racial situation has been transforming in the South, some things have not changed. Larger Southern cities have been opening up to candid discussion on race more readily than small towns in the Deep South. In small Philadelphia, Mississippi, where three civil rights workers were brutally chased down and shot to death in 1964, the situation has improved. But some things have remained the same. For instance, it is a place where supporters of black presidential candidate Barack Obama have not dared to place Obama signs on their lawns. Written before the election, the article asks whether long-held stereotypes in places like Philadelphia, Mississippi, will truly begin to change with the election of a black president.

Some places are defined by a single event. Roswell, N.M., will always be known for space aliens, Lakehurst, N.J., for the *Hindenburg* disaster [when the visiting German airship Hindenburg burned up over a crowd of onlookers]. And [the] little town [of Philadelphia] in the Piney Woods of eastern Mississippi will forever be the site of one of the most brutal crimes of the civil-rights era. But Philadelphia—situated in a rural county once dubbed "Bloody Neshoba"—now can add a footnote to its most nefarious chapter: In the county where three men were murdered for trying to help black people vote, a majority of voters favored putting a black man in the White

House. Much has changed here since black citizens like Sylvia Campbell, now 74, were told they couldn't vote unless they correctly answered how many bubbles were in a bar of soap.

Some Things Do Not Change

But much is the same. For all the excitement about Democratic Sen. Barack Obama of Illinois and his history-making run for president, there is anxiety, too, because the present is still hostage to the past. Everything in this town of more than 80 churches is viewed through the lens of race. Obama's success makes some people as anxious as it makes others proud.

"It's just the impossibility of it," Campbell said.

She had just come from Mount Zion United Methodist, which the Ku Klux Klan once burned down.

"I know Mississippians. Barack Obama will never change the uneducated whites from the South. I don't care what he does. If he's made some of them millionaires, he'll never change them."

Obama's primary victory comes just as Philadelphia prepares to mark the 44th anniversary of the killings. Racial tensions are not as overt today; the slights are subtle, from the glance averted on the street to the job application that is never considered. With five months of presidential campaigning ahead, there is a sense that racial tensions are about to boil again.

"What happened all those years ago—that just keeps coming up," said Doris Gray, 81, who is white.

The presence of the media in her son's chili cafe not 24 hours after Obama cinched the nomination confirmed her fear that people are going to start poking around in matters better left alone. Around here, that always leads to June 21, 1964—Father's Day, to be exact. Mount Zion lay in charred rubble and three civil-rights workers—two white and one black—came to register black voters. The three were stopped by law-enforcement officers and jailed for speeding. Released that night, they were chased down a country road and shot, their bodies found six weeks later in an earthen dam outside town. Seventeen reputed Klansmen were arrested, but only Edgar Ray Killen, a part-time Baptist preacher believed to have masterminded the plan, was charged with murder. An all-white jury deadlocked. The story was fodder for the 1989 movie "Mississippi Burning," which played here at the old State Theatre. A new trial held in 2005 sent the 80-year-old Killen to prison.

With every turn of events, the media converged on Philadelphia, with a population of more than 7,000—55 percent white, 40 percent black. The way it looked to some, everything boomeranged to the town's racist past. Ronald Reagan chose the county fair here to announce his 1980 candidacy for president. Now there's Obama, Philadelphia's most sensitive subject personified.

"I just wish he'd stop talking about race," said Taneil Long, 30, who owns a nail salon.

Running Against the Grain

Many of Long's patrons are black. Ever since word got out seven years ago that she was dating a black man, many white clients deserted Long. Her white landlady told her to move. Her cousin from Memphis, Tenn., hasn't spoken to her since. Long is biracial—part Vietnamese and part white. A Democrat, she likes what Obama has to say, but the subject of race repels her. It runs against the local grain to discuss the matter openly, and it's hard to avoid it whenever Obama comes on TV. She doesn't think an Obama presidency would change the minds of people who haven't changed their minds already.

"It's just unbelievable how hateful some people can be," she said. "If he goes in there and does a remarkable job, maybe some will say, 'Hey, maybe I didn't have the right feeling about that situation.' But as far as Neshoba County goes? You will never get nobody to admit it."

The South of the Old Confederacy is changing, outpacing the rest of the country in population growth and jobs—CNN, Coca-Cola and FedEx are headquartered there. Rural states like Georgia, Florida and Tennessee have more racially tolerant metropolitan centers. But in Deep South states like Mississippi, change has come more slowly. Two Native American casinos outside town have boosted the economy, and Philadelphia, as they say, is fixin' to get a bowling alley. A stronger black leadership has stepped up to demand better police protection and community services, such as equal distribution of parks money, making sure the one in the black neighborhood doesn't get short shrift. James Prince, editor and publisher of the *Neshoba County Democrat*, framed the progress this way: "There are people who, if they could get away with not doing the work in the black park, probably would—but they are not going to get away with it."

Patricia Madison, 39, works at a boutique a few doors from Long's nail salon. It's owned by a young black woman—a departure from how things used to be. Still, Madison, who is black, can point to uneasy moments. A restaurant advertised for a waitress but wouldn't give her a second look. When a white friend invited her to a wedding and the groom's parents objected, she stayed away.

Mississippi's White Voters

Maybe an Obama presidency could help break stubborn stereotypes.

"Maybe people might view us different—see that we are not ignorant. Some of us have class. We can do more than work in the kitchen and be somebody's housekeeper," Madison said.

Just about any adult here has experienced racial prejudice. Steve Wilkerson, a white resident, worked for a service station with one bathroom for men, one for women and one for "coloreds." The first two were cleaned daily; the third once a week.

Now Wilkerson, 55, owns Steven's on the Square, a clothing store. He is a member of a multiracial commission working to heal Philadelphia: The attorney general issued a formal apology, and Highway 19 now bears the names of the civil-rights activists who died there: Andrew Goodman, 20, a white college student from New York; Michael Schwerner, 24, a social worker from New York, and James Chaney, 21, a black man from nearby Meridian.

But Obama's strong performance in a county that is 65 percent white is less a sign of racial tolerance than of white flight to the Republican Party. Those voting on the Democratic side in the primary were mainly blacks or white liberals who tend to be progressive on racial issues. Wilkerson predicted Obama will have a hard time winning Mississippi's white voters in November. Those who do support him will do so discreetly. "They won't have bumper stickers and lawn signs. It would not be comfortable."

Low-Key

Margaret White, 54, stood outside Mount Zion, the church she has attended all her life. It was rebuilt in fire-resistant brick rather than wood. The old bell—all that was left—is in place, and a gray stone engraved with three names stands outside the sanctuary. But there are no high-fives or yelps of Obama's victory. "Low-key is the way," the Rev. Willie Young tells his flock.

White went into work clapping her hands the morning after Obama won [the nomination]. But she didn't flaunt her enthusiasm to white colleagues at Mississippi State University, where she teaches nutrition. "Here, you have to know somebody to get a job," she said. "You can't afford to tick people off." She doesn't hold much hope that Obama's rise will reform old-school Southerners, but she notices the changing attitude of the next generation.

Barack Obama on the presidential campaign trail, addressing supporters at the Mississippi University for Women in Columbus, Mississippi. AP Images.

While neighborhoods remain somewhat segregated, workplaces are diverse, biracial couples common. Children—black and white—play together on sports teams; they not only attend each other's weddings, but take part as bridesmaids and groomsmen. "One day, the old history will just die off and race will still be there, but it won't matter so much," White said.

Race Blindness

Samuel Terence

Samuel Terence is a senior correspondent at The American Prospect.

In the following article, Samuel Terence observes that many of today's African American political leaders have been pursuing race-blind, not race-based, policies. While some blacks have resented this, others have believed it only natural and that, while the world still needs civil rights leaders, black political leaders are politicians who need not be civil rights activists. But while many positive changes have occurred in the African American community, including higher graduation rates and lower poverty, blacks have continued to lag behind whites in these areas. Still, Terence contends, it would be hard for any African American leader to deny that much more is possible for blacks now than in any other time in American history.

On a blustery winter afternoon in January 2005, I went to see Harold Ford Jr. in his congressional office to talk about his upcoming campaign for the U.S. Senate. He guessed he would need about $12 million for the campaign. In terms of actual hurdles, though, he expected to be more disadvantaged by being a Democrat than by being African American.

I was quietly, but completely, blown away.

Had the country changed that much? Was race not the biggest, most confusing totem on the American political horizon? I understood that in 2004 Barack Obama had been elected to the Senate. I understood about the New South. I was in Virginia when Doug Wilder became lieutenant gover-

Samuel Terence, "Young, Black, and Post–Civil Rights," *American Prospect*, vol. 18, September 2007, pp. 23–27.

nor, and I had covered the campaign when he became the first black governor elected in the nation's history. But even with the most generous benefit of the doubt, Ford was still talking about Tennessee, where the Ku Klux Klan was born, where Martin Luther King Jr. died, and where only two black people have ever been elected to Congress, both of them named Harold Ford.

History takes the slow boat and the long way out. Indeed, to the extent that the South has grown increasingly hostile to Democrats for more than a generation, it was the party's positions on race and civil rights that made it so unpalatable to so many Southern whites.

Yet it was clear that Ford, a Southerner, was absolutely serious.

The New Black Leaders

So how much *has* the country changed? This is the question of the moment as we watch the mutations in our national racial DNA triggered by Barack Obama's presidential campaign. Obama, we are reminded constantly, is a singular political talent. But he is in many ways the full flowering of a strain of up-tempo, non-grievance, American-Dream-In-Color politics. His counterparts are young, Ivy League professionals, heirs to the civil-rights movement who are determined to move beyond both the mood and the methods of their forebears.

Where their predecessors went to historically black colleges and universities and often became ministers, this generation of leaders, born in the 1960s and 1970s, went to law school and began building political résumés. Ford went to Penn as an undergrad and law school at Michigan; his father studied mortuary science and went into the family's funeral-home business before going into politics.

These new leaders are not what used to be called race men. They argue, somewhat convincingly, that they don't need to concern themselves primarily with the uplift of their race. They appeal to black voters, to be sure, but to white ones as well. They talk about income inequality, not black unemployment. They rail against inadequate educational opportunities, not the endemic poverty in black neighborhoods that results. They attack globalization and outsourcing, not necessarily the loss of high-wage, low-skill manufacturing jobs that built and sustained large working- and middle-class black communities after World War II.

And they don't want to be just mayors or congressmen from majority-black districts. They want to be governors, senators, and presidents. They look like Ford, Obama, and Deval Patrick, the governor of Massachusetts. They resemble Anthony Brown, the African American lieutenant governor of Maryland, and Artur Davis, a congressman from Alabama, both of whom, like Obama, graduated from Harvard Law School. They look like the Rhodes Scholar mayor of Newark, New Jersey, Cory Booker, who is often accused of not being black enough, and like Adrian Fenty, the new mayor of Washington, D.C., who appointed the first nonblack public-schools chancellor in 40 years. They are mostly Democrats, but they also include a handful of Republicans—Michael Steele, the former lieutenant governor of Maryland, who was the unsuccessful GOP [Republican] nominee for the Senate in 2006, and former Oklahoma Congressman J.C. Watts—who as a matter of ideology have been preaching that the old racial calculus ought to be a less prominent feature in our politics and our lives.

"It is happening as a matter of inevitability," insists Davis, who is considering a run for governor of Alabama in 2010. His odds are long, but more importantly, he is on a short list of very serious candidates, and his race is no longer the inherent bar to victory it once had been.

Preaching Togetherness

Much has changed for the black politician. African Americans, despite their loyalty to the Democrats, are no longer united by the urgent and singular need to end racial injustice. And white

Americans are far more open to black candidates than ever before, opening up a far wider array of public offices than was available a generation ago. This has allowed the new black politician to craft a message that appeals to a broader constituency, a message that is not steeped in race. "Why not talk about the American Dream, that is a dream that is shared by black and white and brown . . . Americans?" asks Brown.

Compelled to reach beyond what is perceived as their natural political base, these candidates and their message may hold the keys to the future of the Democratic Party. It is a message that eschews divisions, particularly racial ones; it taps into an optimism, real or manufactured, that we are all in this together, full of possibility; and it avoids the negative and what detractors call victimhood. Patrick's 2006 campaign slogan in Massachusetts was, "Together We Can," and it is no coincidence that Patrick had the same political consultants as Obama, whose 2004 senate-campaign slogan was, "Yes, We Can."

This is, in essence, the message of the Democratic Party, which has been accused, sometimes fairly, of being less a party than a collection of interest groups. And there may be no more treacherous ground for a Democratic candidate to traverse than addressing the concerns of black voters, crucial to any success, while not seeming beholden to them. Actually, the job may be easier for black Democratic politicians, who can preach togetherness with a reduced burden of having to establish their bona fides with black voters.

Obama is doing all this, but he is not the first. When I met with Ford in 2005, he was 34 and had been elected to the House five times, each time with between 60 percent and 80 percent of the vote, from his majority-black district in Memphis. His father, Harold Ford Sr., had held that seat for 22 years before him. But the younger Ford was moving on, building himself into the prototype crossover black candidate—moderate, affable, eloquent—who would win state and national elections.

It was, after all, four years before Obama's big speech at the 2004 Democratic Convention that Al Gore chose Ford to deliver the keynote address at the party's convention in Los Angeles. Two years later, in a move that many deemed reckless, Ford challenged Nancy Pelosi for party leader in the House. He got crushed, but for someone who had already been thinking about a run for the Senate, it likely did not hurt him at home to take on one of the premier liberal faceplates of the party.

He was a man in full. And despite criticism that he was not progressive enough or that he was in the thrall of a pandering, unprincipled centrism that was killing the Democratic Party, it seemed clear that Ford's was a promising political future. His 2006 campaign was not a sacrificial one. Desperate to retake control of the Senate, Democrats were going to cast their lot with an African American in the South for one of the only open GOP seats of the cycle.

"The race issue is big," he told me, "but the biggest issue I face is being a Democrat."

Questions on Race

Clearly America *has* changed. Who can deny the enormity of racial progress in the 150 years since the Dred Scott decision [of 1856, which claimed since blacks were not citizens they could not bring suit in federal court], or in the 50 years since the Little Rock Nine [when, in 1957, a group of black students enrolled in Little Rock Central School were denied entry by the Arkansas governor], or even in the 15 years since Rodney King [a black taxi driver in Los Angeles who, in 1991, was beaten by police after he was chased for speeding] pleaded helplessly, "Can we all get along?" Ford refers to himself of the "diversity generation" that grew up valuing difference rather than mediating racial strife. They've lived the dream, and represent a generation of black Americans who do not feel cut off from the larger society. Indeed, Obama's raising $33 million in three months is the very definition of this progress.

"The country has evolved on race," Davis says. "I think in the next 15 years there will be six to 10 African Americans who, if their careers take the right turns, will be in position to contend for the presidency. That's breathtaking."

In all likelihood, they will be less liberal and more centrist than those who came before them. Ford opposes gay marriage and supported the war in Iraq. Davis is anti-abortion and pro-gun. Obama, who comes from a liberal city in a Democratic state, also opposes gay marriage, and he angered many progressives and party members when, in his first few weeks in the Senate, the new liberal champion voted for a tort-reform bill that was one of the president's top priorities.

There is open and often bitter speculation about whether this new breed had to pay too great a price for its success, by distancing itself from the causes and crusades that advance the interests of black people. There is little evidence of that in substance, but the shift in tone and perspective troubles some. "The subtext of his appeal is in what he does not say," writer Amina Luqman opined in *The Washington Post*, about Obama's avoidance of difficult historical questions on race. "It's in his ability to declare that things must get better without saying who or what has made them bad. It's how he rarely chastises and how he divides blame and responsibility evenly; white receiving equal parts with black, poor equal parts with rich."

John Conyers, the 40-year House veteran from Detroit, sees them as the organic next step in a long, historic march, but notes that "some of them are not as progressive as they should be from my point of view."

And while Conyers is not among them, there are those who see in that less progressive approach a calculating cynicism to pander to whites by distancing blacks. "Some of these guys have exploited that in a political sense, intentionally or not, to appeal to white voters," says the Rev. Al Sharpton, an old-time agitator.

Still, many say that these political changes are natural and positive development. "They are what we wanted to happen," writer, scholar, and veteran activist Roger Wilkins told the Associated Press about the new black politicians. "You are getting some of the real fruits of the civil-rights movement. I don't view them as in opposition to us; but people born in 1961 see the world differently than people born in 1931."

Race Still an Issue?

If black politicians are allowed to practice a different kind of politics in America today than a generation ago, the reasons can be reduced to two essential factors: Black voters have broader interests and more diverse political demands, and white voters are increasingly open-minded about what their leaders should look like.

African American home ownership is at an all-time high. In 2006, 81 percent of African Americans older than 25 had graduated from high school, compared with 44 percent in 1976, or 28 percent in 1966. Poverty among blacks has dropped from 41.8 percent in 1966 to about 23 percent in 2005. Blacks are the only group among whom voter turnout is rising. And the election of African Americans to public office has taken off: In 1970 there were 1,469 black elected officials in the United States, while today there are more than 9,100. There is no missing the historical irony in the fact that Mississippi, Alabama, and Louisiana top the list of states that have elected the most blacks.

Those officials, in some ways, are evidence of victories in fights that need not be refought. "We could not get past those threshold inclusion issues," says Davis. "We could not be talking about health-care disparities in 1965, when people could not even vote."

But white voters have changed, too, says David Bositis, of the Joint Center for Political and Economic Studies, a think tank in Washington focused on African American issues, and this has allowed African American voters to seek offices representing constituencies much wider that an all-black ward or a majority-black city or congressional district. "White voters have changed so that they are willing to support, and strongly support, black candidates, and black candidates . . . are now offering a vision, an agenda, a politics where they are trying to appeal to all voters, and which more white voters are willing to accept."

In 2006 Ford ran a Senate campaign that appeared to show that race was no longer the dominant and decisive issue it once had been in American political culture—until, that is, race did Ford in. Ford's campaign followed the overall Democratic playbook: He talked about high gas prices, economic unfairness, the failed war in Iraq. Interestingly, when he attacked [President George W.] Bush, he did it from the right, ridiculing the president's immigration plan, for example, as an amnesty for illegal aliens.

And then, with one week to go and the polls putting Ford and his opponent, Bob Corker, in a dead heat, the Republican National Committee put out a television ad showing a young white woman in a strapless dress, announcing: "I met Harold at the Playboy party." Her shoulders bare, she beckoned at the end of the ad, "Harold, call me!" Ford lost by a margin so small—less than 3 percent that any small factor might have made the difference. But the Tennessee campaign is remembered mostly for that ad, which conjured up some of the saddest elements of America's gnarled racial history: The lynching of untold numbers of black men in the South between the end of the Civil War and the end of World War II for crimes, often imagined, that ranged from raping white women to insulting them. The baggage is old, but real and still raw. The effectiveness of the ad depended on one's sense of and sensitivity to history. Clearly it was not meant to evoke morning in America.

Still, Ford emerged from the election with his political bona fides intact and even enhanced. Almost immediately, he talked of another bid for the Senate in 2008. Now he has set his sights on the governor's mansion in Nashville, which will be vacated by term-limited Democrat Phil Bredesen in 2010.

New Politics?

Al Sharpton is calling me back during a break from his radio show. Sharpton is what is casually described as a traditional civil-rights leader. He is definitively old school and savvy enough to understand that when "new generation" black leaders are praised for their "credibility," their "viability," or their ability to "transcend race," the political translation is that they are not Al Sharpton or Jesse Jackson or Louis Farrakhan.

He dismisses the notion that the new politics is all that new. "There have always been black people who worked inside the system, while some worked outside it," he says. "Thurgood Marshall was on the Supreme Court when Martin Luther King was still alive. This ain't generational. Barack Obama and I are the same generation, Deval Patrick and I are the same age." (Sharpton was born in 1954, Patrick in 1956, and Obama in 1961.)

"I think the civil-rights movement has produced leaders who are not civil-rights leaders, but that was the whole point of the civil-rights movement, to give people a chance to live up to their potential," Sharpton says. "The thing that gets me is that when you get some black leaders who are not civil-rights leaders, whether it is Barack Obama or Colin Powell or Tiger Woods, people act like they did that all by themselves, that they opened the door for themselves."

Tensions over the blackness of black candidates have simmered for years, between Booker T. Washington's accomodationist self-help movement and W.E.B. DuBois' more aggressive black activism, between Malcolm X's threats of violence and King's devotion to nonviolence. But today there is something new: "In just my lifetime the meaning of leadership for African Americans has changed," says Congressman Davis. "When my mother came along you could teach, but you couldn't teach white children, you could lead, but you couldn't lead white people. This is a different space. Now you could live up to your potential."

Race-Blind Solutions

The critical question, and it has yet to be answered, is whether living up to one's potential means leaving behind issues that are important to black people. Like the fight for affirmative action, for continued government protection against race-based discrimination in employment, education, housing, and other critical areas. Despite all the measures of progress, African Americans remain a disproportionately large portion of those suffering the ravages on the nation's continued inequality: Three in four white families owned their homes in 2005, while only 46 percent of blacks did; the median income for white households was $50,622 in 2005, while black median household income stood at less than $31,000, a 40 percent disparity that has existed since 1980; and blacks in the United States have an 18.6 percent chance of going to jail at some point in their lives, compared with 3.4 percent for whites.

Nonetheless, the new black politicians seek race-blind, not race-based, solutions. "I can't think of a single issue in American political life where you can still say 'This will exclusively affect blacks,' or 'This will only affect whites,' where you can say what this means for the Black Agenda," says Davis, who admits that in a lot of cases the consequences "fall more acutely on black people."

These new leaders say they leave advocacy for African Americans to civil-rights organizations. Ron Walters, who was the campaign manager on Jesse Jackson's presidential campaign, says that's how it should be. "I think a lot of times people, the media especially, confuse civil-right leaders with political leaders," Waiters said. "The reason African American communities needed civil-rights organizations was because of the injustice and abrogation of rights that existed in our communities. That is not a job for political leaders, and we still need civil-rights leaders." In this division of labor, civil-rights leaders—who have always spent a lot of their effort petitioning political leaders for redress—can now in theory make their case to more highly placed and more sympathetic black leaders.

Everything Is Possible

The emergent strain of American Dream politics from black politicians is attracting a lot of attention at the very moment that some of the civil-rights-era, freedom-fighting types are reaching new heights of political power in the place where historically it has been most significant, the House of Representatives. Last January [2007], Detroit's Conyers, first elected in 1964, became chairman of the House Judiciary Committee. Charles Rangel chairs the powerful Ways and Means Committee, and Mississippi's Bennie Thompson is the new chairman of the Committee of Homeland Security. And before she died in April [2007], California's Juanita Millender-McDonald was head of the Committee on House Administration.

The old guard and the young Turks are mutually respectful, acknowledging that their experiences and opportunities are different because times have changed. "Could you imagine if John Conyers was a 35-year-old lawyer beginning his political career now?" Davis, 39, asked, suggesting that Conyers' political talent today would have taken him beyond the job of veteran congressman.

For his part, Conyers says he is "very enthusiastic about Obama's campaign, because he represents a new dimension to what we saw with Shirley Chisholm, Jesse Jackson, and Al Sharpton," African Americans who ran for president over the past 40 years. "I think it is very critical that we move along with him." . . .

But the true prize for African Americans may be Obama's opportunity to try.

On a rainy, humid afternoon deep in the Alabama summer, people were lined up around the corner, waiting to get into the ballroom of the Sheraton Hotel in downtown Birmingham. More than 2,000 of them paid $25 each to attend an event where they would be served no food, not even a pretzel.

Davis stood on the stage marveling at the crowd. "You have to be from Alabama to appreciate this," he said to Obama, whom he was about to introduce. "I've never seen a more diverse crowd—black, white, rich, poor. It was amazing," he told me later. "That is not the norm in Alabama politics. Usually the black political community tends to do its thing, and the white political community does its thing."

There is a lot of Alabama in Alabama politics. "Not 10 minutes away from that ballroom was the 16th Street Baptist Church where those four little girls got killed in 1963," Davis told me. He asked for a show of hands of people who were around in 1963. There was a sprinkling.

"I bet that you could never have imagined that someone like me would be standing on this stage, getting ready to introduce someone . . ." The crowd erupted. Davis never got to finish the line. "It was astonishing," he recalled later. "To be a black politician born in America after 1960 with the rhetorical skills to communicate a vision to voters, it is possible to have the same career aspirations as white politicians with similar skills," says Davis. "Everything now is in the zone of possibility."

Too Many Blacks Imprisoned

Michael Eric Dyson

Michael Eric Dyson is a professor of sociology at Georgetown University and the author of sixteen books, including April 4, 1968: Martin Luther King Jr.'s Death and How It Changed America, *a* New York Times *best seller.*

As part of the CNN special "Black in America," Michael Eric Dyson told the story of himself and his brother. While Dyson was a university professor and author, his brother was in a jail cell because of a murder charge. While Dyson acknowledged the poor choices his brother had made in his life, he maintained his brother's innocence on the charge of murder. Dyson further claimed that the prison system claimed far too many people of brown and black skin, and that more effort needed to be made to get these individuals out of jails and into schools.

Whenever the segment featuring me and my imprisoned brother, Everett, from Soledad O'Brien's searing CNN special "Black in America" airs nationally, I invariably receive an e-mail, call or comment from a black person saying our story is their story. Not necessarily our particular truth—one brother, an author and professor, the other a prisoner incarcerated with a life sentence—but something close. So many black families are plagued by a similar mathematics of misery: variously stable and prospering members are divided from loved ones behind steel bars and sharply varying educational achievement, bracketed by the cruelly ironic twists of fate. One may teach, as I did for years, at Penn. The other, like my brother, could be locked away in the pen. The temptation is to believe that individual choice alone accounts for such differences in destiny. Successful black family members did their work and played by the rules; suffering family members ran afoul of the law and were justly locked away. Of course, that is true in many cases, but in far too many cases, it's not the entire truth.

Prison or Education?

There is a vicious prison system that hungers for young black and brown bodies. The more young black and brown folk are thrown in jail, the more cells are built, and the more money made. It has been well documented that we spend far more money on penitentiaries than university education for poor black and brown males. During the 1980s and 1990s, state spending for corrections grew at six times the rate of state spending on higher education. By the end of the last century, there were nearly a third more black men in prison and jail than in colleges and universities. That means the number of black men in jail or prison has increased fivefold in the last 20 years. In 1980, at the dawn of the prison construction boom, black men were three times more likely to be enrolled in college than incarcerated. In 2000, there were 791,600 black men in jail or prison, while only 603,032 were enrolled in colleges or universities. In 1980, there were 143,000 black men in jail or prison and 463,700 matriculating in higher educational institutions. In effect, the cellblock or classroom choice is oppressive. We would permit no other population of American citizens to be locked away with such callous disregard for the educational opportunity that might help stem the tide of incarceration.

Everett certainly made self-destructive choices: He sold drugs and admitted he was a pariah to his community. But he is innocent of the charge of murder for which he is serving a life sentence in Michigan. And he is not alone. There are thousands of black men who are rotting in jail cells who have done nothing to merit incarceration. And even when they get

Michael Eric Dyson attends an event on violence against women and girls in New York. Peter Kramer/Getty Images for V-Day

in trouble, a great number of black men go to prison for non-violent drug offenses. Often, crippling racial profiling and suspicion of black men put them on a path to prison, while white males who commit similar offenses are arrested and convicted in far smaller numbers.

The point is not affirmative action for black thugs. The point is that white males often get second, third and fourth chances for reform—either because they weren't suspected to begin with, or they are given far lighter sentences and far more favorable treatment—while black males are severely punished for even relatively small infractions.

The Real Crimes

Besides the choices we made, Everett and I are also examples of an ugly trait that persists in black communities: the ruin of color consciousness. I am a light-skinned brother; Everett is a deep chocolate black man. I am not suggesting that the mere difference in shade has led to his brutal circumstances and my rise. I am arguing, however, that the persistence of colorism—a sometimes subtle hierarchy of social standing historically dictated in part by darkness or lightness of one's skin, measuring the proximity to, or distance from, the vaunted white ideal—affected how he was viewed as a developing youth, impacting the view of what gifts he might possess while shaping the presence or absence of social opportunities open to him. It is true that many darker skinned blacks prosper, and that lighter skinned blacks suffer. But their relative successes and failures are often unconsciously molded in a crucible of race that assigns higher value to the physical features and cultural traits that reflect those of the dominant society.

Everett is a highly intelligent young man who made grievous errors in his life, but none that deserve the fate he presently suffers. It pains me deeply—often, by myself, to tears—to see him suffering so long for a crime that he didn't commit. It hurts as well to know that prisons are being built to fit the failures and struggles of other young black and brown men just like him. I feel an obligation to raise my voice in defense of millions of young black and brown men and women who may one day follow his path. I want to warn them away from the destructive personal habits that make them vulnerable to prison. But I must also cry out against a society that would punish them in such unforgiving fashion while extending mercy to millions more who aren't poor or black.

In my mind, that inequality and injustice are the real crimes.

Transracial Adoptions Still Face Hurdles

Rachel Uranga

Rachel Uranga is a staff writer at the Daily News *in Los Angeles.*

In the following article, Rachel Uranga reports that while more parents have been adopting children of different ethnic backgrounds, many have a continued reluctance to do so. A number of the factors contribute to these parents' reluctance, including the concern that they would not be able to raise racially different children in the tradition of the children's true ethnic background. For those who have adopted across racial lines, their feelings are mixed. While some have made an effort to make the children's ethnicity part of their daily lives, others have not felt it necessary to do so.

It took just a few life-changing seconds for Dane Holweger and Israel Segal to fall in love with Ziggy and Nola. But even with that boundless love, the two know they can't protect their adopted African-American children from racism. As Caucasian men, they just don't have the experience. "I can't raise them as a black parent because I am not black," Holweger said of the 3-year-old twins. "But we are hugely supportive of our children as black children. We want to provide for them culturally."

Heartbreaking Facts

Nearly a decade after Congress forced adoption agencies to throw out race as a deciding factor, the numbers of interracial adoptions have surged. In Los Angeles County, they have

Rachel Uranga, "A Different World After 11 Years, Some Still Opposed to Adopting Kids Across Racial Lines," *Daily News* (Los Angeles), December 18, 2005, p. N1. Copyright © 2007 Los Angeles Newspaper Group. Reproduced by permission.

doubled over the last five years [2001–2005]. Still, the adoption rainbow is hardly idyllic. A debate over the propriety of cross-racial families rages behind closed doors. Some who advocate placing children in same-race families fear that speaking out could cost them federal funds tied to ensuring adoptions are colorblind.

Segal admits that, when he and his partner initially talked about adopting a child of a different race, he was hesitant, even frightened. But more heartbreaking was the long list of African-American boys and Latino siblings who were waiting for adoption. "(Our social worker) said people didn't want children of color, especially boys," said Segal, the son of a Holocaust survivor. "They were kind of afraid of black boys. It shocked me. But once you meet that child, that's the child you want and all that goes out the window."

Los Angeles County officials estimate about 1,200 children are available for adoption at any time. About half are Latino, one-third are African-American, 13 percent are Caucasian and 2 percent are American Indians or Pacific Islanders. And, while critics say a child's most important need is a stable home, many experts insist that adoptive families understand that race—how you look on the outside—shapes identity and how people are judged.

"We often think love will conquer all, but we know that it doesn't," said Maria Quintanilla, executive director of the Latino Family Institute—the only agency in Southern California specializing in placing Latino children.

"First of all, we need to remember that adoption is created through loss," Quintanilla said. "(Children) are already coming in with multiple losses—their siblings, their neighborhoods. And, on top of that, they are losing their culture, their history."

"It's one loss after the other."

Colorblind Placements

For much of the 1970s and '80s, social workers in major metropolitan areas favored same-race adoption. But then came the 1989 case of Maurice West, a 2-year-old African-American who was taken from a white foster home in Ohio and adopted by an African-American couple in New York. Eight weeks later, the toddler died of repeated beatings by his adoptive parents. That case prompted then-U.S. Sen. Howard Metzenbaum of Ohio to sponsor the Multi-Ethnic Placement Act, which prevents race from becoming the primary factor in determining placement. The 1994 rule was amended two years later to prohibit agencies from considering race at all, essentially ensuring agencies are colorblind.

Social workers could no longer delay or deny an adoption because of race and, in some cases, couldn't talk about ethnicity with families. But the bill also required greater recruitment in communities with adopted children. "The feeling was that agencies were not placing kids from foster care in families because they couldn't locate enough families (of the same race)," said Kate Cleary, executive director of Consortium for Children, a San Rafael, Calif.–based group that mediates open adoptions. "They thought we would see loads of kids adopted . . . because they removed this artificial barrier. The effect has been negligible. We still have huge numbers of kids waiting for families."

Recently, the Department of Children and Family Services has expanded recruitment in African-American and Latino churches. The department also is partnering with faith-based groups to feature an adoptable child in the church bulletin and is training adoptive parents how to recruit other would-be parents. But some like Quintanilla say the department still has this ideal of what a family should look like and don't have enough outreach in the Latino community.

Maintaining Family Ties

"Who is gorgeous?" Israel Segal coos as he hugs Ziggy. The toddler giggles, dropping his head to his chest, then quickly peeking at his dad.

"Who is gorgeous?" Segal repeats, tickling the little boy as he wiggles around.

More giggles.

"Not me," Ziggy replies, with a wide smile. "Nooollllllaaa," he says pointing to his sister.

The twins are very close, and Segal hopes they'll remain that way so they can help each other deal with cultural questions as they grow older. The couple has also found support in the black community and has promised to attend holiday functions hosted by the African-American family that adopted the twins' half-sisters and half-brothers. While Segal and Holweger make an extra effort to bridge the racial gap, others hardly give it a thought. Bertha Monroy, a 57-year-old Salvadorean immigrant, says she really never considered the heritage of her two African-American children until somebody brought it up. "Briona was something very special," she said of the 5-year old African-American girl who arrived at her house [in 2004]. "She came with marks (of abuse) on her body. Somebody did something very terrible. I started to love her." And vice versa. Briona picked up Spanish within two weeks and clung to Monroy, staying up late to clean up the North Hollywood house. "She says, 'Mommy, I want to help you with dishes.' I had to pretend to go to sleep so she would fall asleep. She stole my heart."

On the day of adoption, another foster mother caring for Briona's older sister met the olive-skinned Monroy at the court. "She told me, 'What are you going to do with a black girl?' and I said, 'Listen to me. I am black, too. Don't you see my color skin?' . . . I was so angry." She eventually adopted Briona, as well as her elder sister Tatina. She learned from a friend how to take care of the girls' hair and skin. But, she said, she is not going out of her way to go to certain churches or expose them to different people because the girls are black. Instead, she said, she will wait for them to lead the way. "They are human and similar to me," she said. "One day they are going to decide to go to their neighborhood and if they want me to go then I will follow." It's perhaps the best move a parent could make, stepping back.

Not Always Easy

"This is not a walk in the park," said Mei Lin Kroll, a 30-year-old West Los Angeles loan officer, who is the adopted daughter of Joe Kroll, executive director of North American Council on Adoptable Children. She was just 3 when her parents adopted her through an international Korean adoption agency.

As a youth, they enrolled her in Korean culture camp, signed her up for a preteen Korean group and made lifelong friends with a Korean-American baby sitter who taught her the Korean language. But they couldn't stop children from teasing her about her flat face or small eyes. And, in the end, that was fine with Kroll, because they let her learn for herself. "Sometimes my parents didn't have answers for things . . . but they realized there was nothing they could do."

Defined by Hip-Hop

Keli Goff

Keli Goff is an author and political analyst whose views have been heard on numerous television and radio stations.

In the following article, Keli Goff contends that while previous generations were defined by major cultural events that bound people together—there were world wars, the Great Depression, the Civil Rights Movement—today's youth have had no such identifiable landmark. But for the past two decades, the hip-hop movement has filled this void, Goff argues, often replacing youth's need for political systems. While hip-hop has reached both black and white youth, Goff points out that the meaning of hip-hop is not the same for a white suburban teen as for an black urban teen.

Every generation is defined by something. For Americans born at the turn of the twentieth century, it was World War I. For their children, it was the Great Depression and World War II. And for their children's children—baby boomers—it was Vietnam, Watergate, and of course, the civil rights movement.

For black Americans, the civil rights movement was more than one defining moment among many. Regardless of wealth, social status, or geographic location, there is not a black American born anytime before 1960 whose life was not forever changed by it.

Now, nearly four decades after the right to vote became more than an impossible dream for many African Americans, we may see yet another impossible dream come true. A black man may actually be elected president. This reality (the very

Keli Goff, *Party Crashing: How the Hip-Hop Generation Declared Political Independence*. Cambridge, MA: BasicCivitas Books, 2008. Copyright © 2008 by Keli Goff. Reprinted by permission of CIVITAS, a member of Perseus Books, L.L.C.

thought of which probably would have caused most southern politicians to laugh to the point of tears forty years ago) raises the question of what is the defining experience for the generation of black Americans who have come of age in post–civil rights America.

Unlike previous generations that were defined by one or two major cultural touchstones, the post–civil rights generation cannot point to a single unifying experience. Instead, it has been shaped by a variety of cultural landmarks, some triumphant, others tragic: the war on drugs, the war in Iraq, 9/11, the rise of hip-hop, the rise of Oprah [Winfrey], the deaths of [rappers] Tupac [Shakur] and Biggie [Smalls], and the presidential campaigns of Jesse Jackson and Barack Obama.

What it has not experienced is legal segregation. This single fact has had a profound impact on the way the post–civil rights generation views politics.

Youth Identity Today and Yesterday

The success of the civil rights movement gained black Americans countless rights, big and small—from equality in access to education and housing to water fountains—and yet it stripped black Americans of one historic privilege: the ability to share an inherent social and political bond. As Bakari Kitwana notes in his landmark book *The Hip Hop Generation*, "The previous generation had the luxury (if you want to call it that) of a broad-based movement. In a climate that screamed for change, youth movements across race, class, gender, and ethnicity were part of the culture."

That isn't so any more. Post–civil rights black Americans are not defined by a universal social or political cause or movement as their parents and grandparents once were. Despite the best efforts of political strategists and the media to pigeonhole them, younger black Americans are staking out their own social and political identities. For some, this means embracing specific labels. Others simply want to be recognized by a political label that has long eluded black Americans: voter.

Not black voter. Not young black voter. Just voter.

But labels are often irresistible, and Kitwana has helped name this generation for the music and culture that many believe most sets them apart: the Hip-Hop Generation. Born between 1965 and 1984, one could argue that this is a group for whom [hip-hop group] Public Enemy's "Fight the Power" is as much an anthem as "We Shall Overcome" [a protest song of the civil rights era] was for their parents.

Hip-Hop: A Cultural Force

Love it or hate it, hip-hop has been one of the defining cultural forces of the last two decades. Once a staple of the inner-city streets, today the music of 50 Cent or Yung Joc is just as likely to be heard blasting in the suburban homes of affluent white kids, in some cases even more so. For some, hip-hop music and culture embodies the essence of their American experience—in which to struggle is a fact of life and protest and rebellion are the only ways to be heard. Therefore hip-hop embodies the essence of their political identity. Others view it as merely one aspect of African American culture, not the most important aspect or the one that defines their American experience or political identity. The struggle of young black Americans to reconcile these two views is at the heart of the politics of the post–civil rights generation.

Like the blues before it, hip-hop is more than an art form. It is the soundtrack to the triumphs and tragedies of this generation's experience; but unlike blues or rock, hip-hop transcends the boundaries of music. While some (like my mother) dismiss it as questionable words put to indistinguishable beats, it has left an indelible mark on American culture, from fashion and film to politics.

Sean "P. Diddy" Combs on a "Vote or Die" Citizen Change Tour stop at Temple University during the 2004 presidential election. Joseph Labolito/Wire Image/Getty Images.

The Voice of Hip-Hop

Hip-hop's reach into mainstream popular culture, as well as the lack of a definitive, unifying political movement among younger black Americans, may explain why a name initially limited to a section in a CD store has come to be applied to a whole generation. Following the first ever hip-hop political convention, the *Black Commentator* wrote, "In the absence of a mass Black political movement, the generation born after 1965 has been named for the culture it created, rather than—as with the preceding generation—the political goals for which they fought."

This has turned out to be both a blessing and a curse. On the one hand, it has given a voice to a generation that might otherwise have been ignored by society altogether. On the other hand there are many who do not deem hip-hop's contribution to be especially positive. As Kitwana notes, "It is not uncommon to hear some of these community leaders dismiss rap music—the most significant cultural achievement of our generation—as ghetto culture. Most of our parents, and especially civil rights leaders and community activists, would rather ignore rap's impact—especially those lyrics that delve into the gritty street culture of the Black underworld—than explore its role in the lives of hip-hop generationers." Today, however, the negative rap on hip-hop no longer falls strictly along generational lines.

The controversy surrounding radio personality Don Imus's comments about the Rutgers women's basketball team, in which he referred to them as "nappy headed hos," cast a spotlight on how increasingly divisive the content of hip-hop music and the image its culture represents have become among black Americans. The argument lobbed by Imus defenders, sometimes with excessive enthusiasm, went something like this: if a twenty-something rapper can call a black woman "ho" in a song, why can't a sixty-something white guy say it in good fun?

Yet long before the Imus controversy, a growing number of black Americans of the so-called Hip-Hop Generation had begun to question whether hip-hop was doing more harm than good. Students at historically black Spelman College have been among the most vocal critics of hip-hop's often negative depiction of young black women, although their crusade was overlooked by most mainstream news outlets until Imus made the issue of interest to mainstream America. Following the Imus brouhaha, Oprah Winfrey devoted two episodes of her program to a town hall discussion among cultural critics of hip-hop, students at Spelman, and prominent figures within the hip-hop community such as [leading hip-hop producer] Russell Simmons and [hip-hop record executive] Kevin Liles, one of the highest-ranking African Americans in the music industry.

Hip-Hop Audience

While [music] critics like Stanley Crouch liken hard-core rap to a modern-day "minstrel show" in which white suburban teens go on "audio safari" to see "darkies in their element,"

Simmons and Liles argue that hip-hop reflects the gritty reality of everyday life in impoverished communities. As is often the case with controversial subjects, the truth is likely somewhere in the middle.

As hip-hop struggles through growing pains, its audience has already begun to move on. The latest music industry sales figures suggest that hip-hop's reign as a defining cultural arbiter may be coming to a close. According to [music sales information system] Nielsen Soundscan, sales of rap music fell by 21 percent in 2006. In our survey of four hundred randomly selected black Americans ages eighteen to forty-five, 19 percent identified themselves as *not* fans of hip-hop, while 47 percent said they listen to it but believe "most of it reflects negatively on black Americans." A discussion regarding the current state of hip-hop music is relevant to a larger discussion regarding the state of political activism among young black Americans.

While hip-hop's emergence as a cultural force is indisputable, its success in the past ten years has been due in large part to a cult-like following among suburban white teens. Yet the political agenda that moves a nineteen-year-old white teen living in Beverly Hills is unlikely to be the same one that moves a nineteen-year-old black teen in the Bronx. Lumping the two under the same political umbrella simply because of similar CD collections is absurd.

Hip-Hop Generation

Kitwana says he coined the term "Hip-Hop Generation" largely in reaction to media attempts to lump post–baby boomer black Americans under the label Generation X, a formula he considers inaccurate and irresponsible because the experiences and concerns of many young black Americans is so different from their white counterparts. But just as the Gen X label and what it came to represent (grunge music, the dot-com boom, the film *Reality Bites*, and "finding yourself") cannot fully capture the diverse experiences of that generation, the term "Hip-Hop Generation" fails to capture the broad experiences of young black Americans, or the range of their political philosophies. How can the political ideology of an entire generation be defined by a music and a culture that many members of that generation believe does not represent them?

Alexis McGill is a political scientist and consultant who has worked extensively with "hip-hop voters," first with Russell Simmons and his political group, the Hip-Hop Summit Action Network, and later with hip-hop mogul and rapper Sean "Diddy" Combs and his political group Citizen Change. McGill is not surprised by the media and political establishment's efforts to paint all younger blacks with a broad brush. Historically, she says, "I don't think we've made the argument that the black community is not monolithic, and so the media cuts to representations they have easiest access to."

While Kitwana recognizes that "there are many people within the quote unquote hip-hop generation who are not defined by that," he asserts that the labeling reflects "what hip-hop has done [to] organize young people at a national and international level." From Kitwana's perspective, hip-hop has served as a mechanism for mobilizing an entire generation around issues that matter to them, inspiring people on a national and international level in a way that "is unprecedented." Beyond providing a platform for artistic expression, hip-hop has "created a national political infrastructure."

This infrastructure grew largely out of grassroots activism among young, predominantly black Americans who were brought together by a shared love of hip-hop but were also united by their distrust of the traditional political process and politicians. A lot of these people, says Kitwana, "see electoral politics as bullshit, a waste of time, orchestrated, not going to bring about any tangible change, and you hear that from artists like Talib Kweli or the rapper Nas, and they represent a sentiment that is out there."

No Faith in the Political System

The sentiment is so widespread that it has sounded panic alarms among Democrats, not because they fear losing members of the Hip-Hop Generation to the GOP [Republican Party] but losing them, period. "When you look at statistics among younger African American men, they are becoming a real hard target for turnout, because they are dropping out of [the] participation process at a higher rate than are young African American women. Part of that is their cynicism and frustration about politics is higher," says Cornell Belcher, head pollster for the Democratic National Committee [DNC].

Basil Smikle, Jr., a member of the post–civil rights generation and a political veteran, concurs. A political consultant whose career has included stints as a senior aide to Senator Hillary Rodham Clinton and an adviser to the presidential campaign of Senator Joseph Lieberman, Smikle says, "People are falling out of the political process because nobody actually thinks politics helps them." While it is a problem for both major parties, he predicts that it will be an even greater problem for Democrats. Due to rising dropout rates, joblessness, and incarceration, young black men are becoming increasingly alienated from mainstream society as a whole, and thus their political involvement down the line becomes less and less likely. Smikle believes this combination of factors means that Democrats will end up "losing a significant part of the base."

Assemblyman Adam Clayton Powell IV is a second-generation black elected official. His father, Adam Clayton Powell, Jr., was one of the first black congressmen of the modern era. Powell explains that part of the problem is that older black leaders and other elected officials struggle to reach young black voters. "The Hip-Hop Generation," Powell notes, "has practically dominated everything from culture, music, economics" but adds that "they dominate everything except politics, because they generally have not been participating."

Cornell Belcher, the DNC pollster, says that "the real issue is they're not seeing politics first and foremost as the most viable avenue for bringing about change in the community, in their community; the change they desperately want to bring about." He adds, "You have younger African Americans, particularly younger African American males, searching for viable vehicles to bring about change."

Hip-Hop Profiling

Kitwana observes that many members of the Hip-Hop Generation feel that the mainstream political establishment ignores the issues that most affect them, like police brutality and what he terms "hip-hop profiling": young black men being targeted for the way they dress, a problem he says is even more prevalent than racial profiling. For many this sentiment has been reinforced by two recent high-profile cases.

The case of six teens from Louisiana, dubbed the Jena Six, galvanized young black Americans, as did the case of homecoming king turned inmate, Genarlow Wilson. While a far cry from the days of Emmett Till [a 14-year-old boy killed in Mississippi for whistling at a white woman in 1955] both cases were steeped in racial overtones. In the case of the Jena Six, one black teenager initially faced nearly twenty years in prison after he and five others were accused of assaulting a white classmate. The incident followed a series of racially charged clashes that began when nooses were found hanging from a tree on their high school campus. In Georgia seventeen-year-old Genarlow Wilson, who is also African American, was sentenced to a mandatory minimum ten years in prison after being convicted of aggravated child molestation for engaging in consensual oral sex with a fifteen-year-old.

Both cases prompted a public outcry and accusations of racial bias. While debate continues regarding the details of the Jena Six case, critics have noted that the white students accused of the noose incident faced minimal punishment for what was deemed a prank. The black students, however, faced the possibility of serious prison time. The national attention both cases garnered (fueled in large part by the efforts of young black Americans) is credited with pressuring local authorities to revisit the cases, resulting in Wilson's release in 2006 after more than two years behind bars. Mychal Bell, the only member of the Jena Six to have been tried at the time of this writing, had his initial conviction set aside on the grounds that he should have been tried as a juvenile, not an adult, for the reduced charges of aggravated battery and conspiracy. (Bell originally faced charges of attempted murder.)

Not All Racism Is Overt

Genarlow Wilson's attorney, B.J. Bernstein, who is white, discusses the role that "subtle racism" played in her client's case. Drawing a distinction between "overt" racism, Bernstein notes that contrary to some media reports Wilson's alleged victim is not white but African American. Despite this fact, Bernstein acknowledges that racial stereotypes ultimately played a role in her client's prosecution. In an interview with CNN she recalls hearing various lawmakers refer to Wilson, an honor student, as a "thug," a perception buoyed by video taken at the scene of the alleged crime. "They see the videotape. There is rap music. Genarlow had dreads at the time. He was a great student, but he looked like a thug on a music video. And, at the legislative session, you heard them say, oh, he is just a thug." As Bernstein astutely observes, were it not for its amateurish quality, the video of Wilson really wouldn't look that different from your typical rap video—just a couple of guys chillin' with a couple of girls. The key difference of course is that the fantasy Wilson and the other young men appear to be living on camera turned into the ultimate nightmare. Wilson, in spite of his numerous non-thug-like accomplishments, became a victim of the "hip-hop profiling" Kitwana speaks of, because when many people viewed the video they didn't see Genarlow Wilson homecoming king or honor student; they simply saw a "thug."

Limited Opportunities

In addition to being wary of law enforcement, Kitwana argues that many members of this generation are also inherently distrustful of traditional social institutions. Globalization, the increasing instability of the American workforce, and the war on terror have given them a sense of unease, as they have grown up in a much less stable world than the one baby boomers and the civil rights generation grew up in. "If you look at someone born in the mid- to late 1960s, if they are born to parents who are not college educated—and even some whose parents are—there are very few options. If they go to college they are already part of an elite group." But those not fortunate enough to go to college (and given that in some major cities as many as half of young black males do not finish high school, there are many) end up with "McJobs" (as in low-wage service jobs at McDonald's) or "working at Wal-Mart or something." Or they hit what many view as the ultimate jackpot and "become a rapper or a basketball player."

But a more realistic possibility is that they will not end up in Wal-Mart or the NBA but in prison. According to a 2005 report by the National Urban League, "One in 20 black men are incarcerated, while one in 155 white men are, and for every three black men in college, four are incarcerated."

Even ten years ago, Kitwana adds, joining the military was considered a viable option. He wryly notes that he was fortunate to attend high school in the "be all you can be" era, in which commercials made the military look like a great way to pay for college, meet girls, and make Mom proud. "There weren't any real major conflicts. You could go into the military and make it into a career and not have any real threat of

war. Whereas for younger members of the Hip-Hop Generation, the threat of war is ever present."

These limited opportunities contrast greatly with those
available to this generation's parents, for whom the rules were
relatively clear: work hard for the same employer for a lifetime
and you will get a piece of the Americans Dream, maybe not a
huge piece, but enough to buy a home and raise a family, and
enough to retire on. "These things absolutely define our politics. If you grow up having a clear understanding of these limited options, it makes you feel very cynical. It makes you feel
like the older generation of our country is not looking out for
you." He believes that this cynicism will continue to have a
profound ripple effect on the traditional political process,
most notably in driving members of the Hip-Hop Generation
farther and farther away from traditional politics. "One of the
things that comes with this generation is cynicism about the
government's ability to seriously intervene in the lives of everyday people. I think this generation has the idea that government is something that works for rich people; something
that works for corporations because that's how we've seen the
government."

For Further Discussion

1. In Chapter 1, Edward D. Clark asserts that Richard Wright "experienced some of the most severe abuses of racial oppression in Mississippi." While this is likely true, Wright's move to the North did not eliminate racism in his life. As Hazel Rowley points out: "He had left behind racist brutality of the South, but the humiliations of the North were almost harder to bear, because they were more capricious." From your reading of Chapter 1 and of *Native Son*, compare and contrast the differences between southern racism and northern racism in 1930s America. Using essays in Chapter 3 and other current news sources, describe how the situation in both the North and the South has changed since the 1930s. Has anything remained the same? Explain your answer.

2. In Chapter 2, both James Baldwin and Irving Howe recognize as a possible flaw *Native Son*'s failure to portray significant relationships among African Americans. As Baldwin puts it, "The relationship that Negroes bear to one another, that depth of involvement and unspoken recognition of shared experience which creates a way of life" was not to be found in *Native Son*. Although Howe disagrees with Baldwin's other criticisms of *Native Son*, he supports this argument: "There can be little doubt that in this respect Baldwin did score a major point. . . ." From your reading of these two essays and of *Native Son*, do you agree with Baldwin and Howe? Why or why not? How would the inclusion of the shared traditions and understandings among African Americans have changed the mood of *Native Son*?

3. The first three essays in Chapter 2 reflect an ongoing literary argument among the writers (James Baldwin, Irving Howe, and Ralph Ellison). What are the main differences in the way each perceives *Native Son* and Richard Wright? Do you believe the race of each writer (Howe is white; Baldwin and Ellison are black) is a significant factor in their arguments? Why or why not? Do Howe, Baldwin, and Ellison think it is significant? Explain your answer.

4. In Chapter 2, both Joseph T. Skerrett Jr. and Lale Demirtürk argue that, in killing Mary Dalton, Bigger felt a sense of power over whites for the first time in his life. Provide evidence of this from Skerrett's and Demirtürk's essays. Why did killing Mary leave Bigger with a sense of power over whites? How does this reinforce Stephen George's assertion that Bigger is "a monstrous symbol of what could happen nationwide if society refuses to make the American dream of freedom and opportunity open to all"?

5. In Chapter 3, Samuel Terence claims African Americans "are no longer united by the urgent singular need to end racial injustice." Keli Goff concurs, stating that "unlike previous generations that were defined by one or two major cultural touchstones, the post–civil rights generation cannot point to a single unifying experience." But while Terence focuses on how this has led to black political leaders steering away from race-based politics, Goff points out how, for young voters, this void has been filled by the culture of hip hop. Do the two arguments here identify a possible fracture in the relationship between black politicians and young black voters? Explain your answer. Do you believe political decisions should be race-based or race-blind? Why? Do you think the current hip-hop culture reflects a realistic perspective of the social and political climate of our country? Why or why not? Use evidence from Terence's and Goff's essays, in addition to other current news, in your answers.

For Further Reading

Richard Wright, *American Hunger*. New York: Harper & Row, 1977.

———, *Black Boy*. New York: Harper & Bros., 1945.

———, *Eight Men*. Cleveland: World, 1961.

———, *A Father's Law*. London: HarperPerennial, 2008.

———, *Lawd Today!* New York: Walker, 1963.

———, *The Long Dream*. Garden City, NY: Doubleday, 1958.

———, *The Outsider*. New York: Harper, 1953.

———, *Rite of Passage*. New York: HarperCollins, 1994.

———, *12 Million Black Voices: A Folk History of the Negro in the United States*. New York: Viking, 1941.

———, *Uncle Tom's Children*. New York: Harper & Bros., 1938.

Bibliography

Books

Richard Abcarian, ed.
Richard Wright's "Native Son": A Critical Handbook. Belmont, CA: Wadsworth, 1970.

Houston Baker
Twentieth Century Interpretations of "Native Son." Englewood Cliffs, NJ: Prentice-Hall, 1972.

David Bakish
Richard Wright. New York: Ungar, 1973.

Russell C. Brignano
Richard Wright: An Introduction to the Man and His Works. Pittsburgh: University of Pittsburgh Press, 1970.

Robert Butler
"Native Son": The Emergence of a New Black Hero. Boston: Twayne, 1991.

Michel Fabre
The Unfinished Quest of Richard Wright. New York: Morrow, 1973.

Michel Fabre
The World of Richard Wright. Jackson: University Press of Mississippi, 1985.

Robert Felgar
Richard Wright. Boston: Twayne, 1980.

Irving Howe
A World More Attractive: A View of Modern Literature and Politics. New York: Horizon, 1963.

Randall Kennedy	*Race, Crime, and the Law*. New York: Pantheon, 1997.
Keneth Kinnamon and Michel Fabre, eds.	*Conversations with Richard Wright*. Jackson: University Press of Mississippi, 1993.
John M. Reilly	*Richard Wright: The Critical Reception*. New York: B. Franklin, 1978.
Samuel Walker, Cassia Spohn, and Miriam DeLone	*The Color of Justice: Race, Ethnicity, and Crime in America*. Belmont, CA: Wadsworth, 1996.
John Williams and Dorothy Sterling	*The Most Native of Sons: A Biography of Richard Wright*. Garden City, NY: Doubleday, 1970.

Periodicals

Sheldon Brivic	"Conflict of Values: Richard Wright's *Native Son*," *Novel*, Spring 1974.
Jerry H. Bryant	"The Violence of *Native Son*," *Southern Review*, April 1981.
CNN	"Being Black Can Mean Being a Suspect," July 24, 2008.
Debra Dickerson	"Racist Like Me," *Slate*, August 11, 2004. www.slate.com.
Laurel J. Gardner	"The Progression of Meaning in Images of Violence in Richard Wright's *Uncle Tom's Children* and *Native Son*," *CLA Journal*, June 1995.

Cynthia Gordy   "Extreme Lockup: Why Are So Many of Our Young Children Being Treated Like Criminals?" *Essence*, December 2007.

Sharon Hamilton   "Wright's *Native Son*," *Explicator*, Summer 1997.

Blyden Jackson   "Richard Wright: Black Boy from America's Black Belt and Urban Ghettos," *CLA Journal*, June 1969.

George E. Kent   "Richard Wright: Blackness and the Adventure of Western Culture," *CLA Journal*, June 1969.

Maxine L. Montgomery   "Racial Armageddon: The Image of Apocalypse in Richard Wright's *Native Son*," *CLA Journal*, June 1991.

Alexander Nejako   "Bigger's Choice: The Failure of African-American Masculinities in *Native Son*," *CLA Journal*, June 2001.

Obioma Nnaemeka   "Richard Wright: Climate of Fear and Violence," *Western Journal of Black Studies*, Spring 1992.

Kathleen Ochshorn   "The Community of *Native Son*," *Mississippi Quarterly*, Fall 1989.

Dean Ornish   "The Toxic Power of Racism," *Newsweek*, March 25, 2008.

Dorothy Redden   "Richard Wright and *Native Son*: Not Guilty," *Black American Literature Forum*, Winter 1976.

Faye McDonald   "Crime Is Too Close," *Essence*, August
Smith   1992.

Victoria Valentine "Youth Crime, Adult Time," *Emerge*,
                    October 1998.

Frederic Wertham   "An Unconscious Determinant in
                    Native Son," *Journal of Clinical
                    Psychopathy and Psychotherapy*,
                    Winter 1944.

Howard Witt   "When Hate Crime Is Not a Black
                    and White Issue," *Seattle Times*, June
                    11, 2007.

Index